# STREETS RECONSIDERED

*Inclusive Design for the Public Realm*

*Streets Reconsidered* is a fundamental rethinking of America's streets. It explores what America's roadways could offer if they were designed for living, along with driving. What if streets accommodated people of all ages and abilities using all travel modes and promoted healthy urban living, social interaction, business and regeneration of the environment? This book pushes beyond the current standards, focusing on planning, designing and constructing streets that improve our built environment for everyone.

The book examines the true functions of a street through case studies from around the world, and includes design guidelines and best practices. City planners, policymakers, urban designers, developers, architects and landscape architects—and community members who share a passion for great urban, human spaces—this book has been written for you.

**Daniel Iacofano**, PhD., FAICP, FASLA, has over 30 years of experience in regional and land use planning and community-based urban planning and design. Dr. Iacofano has worked with hundreds of communities across the United States, helping them strategically plan for positive change. He has consulted and lectured throughout the United States, Europe and Japan, and has written many other books about the built environment. His work has been honored by the National League of Cities, the International Downtown Association, American Planning Association, American Society of Landscape Architects and Association of Environmental Professionals. He is a founding principal and CEO of MIG, Inc.

**Mukul Malhotra** has over 20 years of experience in urban design, planning and architecture in India and the United States. Mr. Malhotra is one of the creators of "re:Streets," the multidisciplinary collaboration focused on planning, designing and constructing streets as a method for improving the built environment for everyone. He has worked with an array of cities, agencies and community groups across the United States to sustainably redevelop urban and neighborhood corridors and streetscapes. His work has been honored by the American Public Works Association, American Society of Landscape Architects, and American Planning Association. He is a principal of MIG, Inc.

DAISY GREEN
daisygreen95@hotmail.co.uk

~~~

# STREETS RECONSIDERED

*Inclusive Design for the Public Realm*

Daniel Iacofano & Mukul Malhotra

ROUTLEDGE

First published 2019
by Routledge
52 Vanderbilt Avenue, New York, NY 10017
and by Routledge
2 Park Square, Milton Park, Abingdon, Oxon, OX14 4RN
Routledge is an imprint of the Taylor & Francis Group, an informa business

British Library Cataloguing-in-Publication Data
A catalogue record for this book is available from the British Library
Library of Congress Cataloging-in-Publication Data
Names: Iacofano, Daniel S., author. | Malhotra, Mukul, author.
Title: Streets reconsidered : inclusive design for the public realm / Daniel Iacofano & Mukul Malhotra.
Description: New York, NY : Routledge, 2019.
Identifiers: LCCN 2018033832 (print) | LCCN 2018036299 (ebook) | ISBN 9781315707273 (e-book) |
ISBN 9781138900424 (hbk) | ISBN 9781138900431 (pbk) | ISBN 9781315707273 (ebk)
Subjects: LCSH: Urban transportation. | Grid plans (City planning) | Neighborhood planning. |
Traffic engineering. | Street life. | Streets--Design and construction.
Classification: LCC HE148 (ebook) | LCC HE148 .I23 2019 (print) | DDC 388.1--dc23
LC record available at https://lccn.loc.gov/2018033832
ISBN: 978-1-138-90042-4 (hbk)
ISBN: 978-1-138-90043-1 (pbk)
ISBN: 978-1-315-70727-3 (ebk)

Typeset in Chaparral Pro and Myriad Pro by MIG, Inc.

Publisher's Note: This book has been prepared from camera-ready copy provided by the author.

*To Susan...*
*Our friend, colleague, partner and teacher...*

## ACKNOWLEDGEMENTS

This book has been a long labor of conversations, visions, arguments, consensus—and many trips back and forth across the country. It began with a glimmer of an idea of how streets, which take up so much of our space, could be so much more than what they are. In 2011, we held the first re:Streets charrette here in Berkeley; ten more followed nationwide. We gathered the ideas of hundreds of professionals about the benefits streets can offer communities; we are grateful for all their contributions. We'd like to thank our MIG colleagues who ran "test kitchens" designing and implementing our often unorthodox concepts; they always make our ideas even better in reality. We would also like to note the MIG creative team that turned thoughts and ideas and into a compelling book: writer Joyce Vollmer, art director Carie DeRuiter, designer Sara Raffo, production designer Catherine Courtenaye, streetscape designer Rishi Dhody, photographer Billy Hustace and illustrator Markus Lui. Thank you.

*Daniel Iacofano*

I owe thanks to many people. To mom and dad, for always loving and inspiring me. To my brother, who has always been there for me. To my professors at Cal, who taught me to ask "why" before jumping to a solution. A special thanks to Allan Jacobs, who was the first person to tell me to believe in myself. To Susan, who taught me to stop complaining and to channel my complaints and frustrations into getting my crazy designs and dreams built; I will always remember the scoldings and the conversations during our long car rides. To Daniel, who taught me the value of planning and to have a vision. The journey to build a different kind of street across the country, test new ideas and convince people to embrace change would have been impossible without his leadership and support. And to Joyce, who transforms words and facts into memorable stories that appeal to everyone; thank you for patience and creativity. This book would not be possible without her help.

*Mukul Malhotra*

**re:Streets Project Advisory Group 2010–2012**

Chris Beynon, Board of Directors, International Downtown Association (IDA) and Principal, MIG, Inc.

Maggie Campbell, President, Partnership for Downtown St. Louis

Tim Gilbert, Board of Directors, America Walks; Liaison to Complete Streets Coalition

Susan Goltsman, Co-Founder and Principal, MIG, Inc.

Daniel Iacofano, Co-Founder and CEO, MIG, Inc.

Elizabeth Macdonald, Department of City and Regional Planning, UC Berkeley

Mukul Malhotra, Director of Urban Design and Principal, MIG, Inc.

Rock Miller, Vice President, Institute of Transportation Engineers (ITE)

Anne Nelson, Environmental Program Coordinator, Bureau of Environmental Services, City of Portland

Norm Steinman, Director, Department of Transportation, City of Charlotte, North Carolina

This project was funded in part by a grant from the National Endowment for the Arts.

CONTENTS

# 1

## THE WORLD ON THE STREET

*Introduction*

We used to grow up on the street. We'd play, we'd walk to neighbors with a casserole for the block potluck, we'd ride bikes, play games, hang out, socialize. So would our pets. Drivers knew enough to watch out for us. We all survived and thrived. We want that again.

So let's design streets for living, not just driving. That's the basic premise of this book: reconsider America's public realm—going the next step beyond travel lanes and bike lanes, sidewalks and crosswalks. Let's rediscover all the benefits that streets can offer communities.

PREVIOUS: West Capitol Avenue, Sacramento. Project design and photo by MIG, Inc. FACING: Nueva Street, San Antonio. Project design and photo by MIG, Inc. ABOVE RIGHT: Lincoln Highway between Gettysburg and Chambersburg, Pennsylvania, 1921. Photo courtesy The Lincoln Highway Digital Image Collection, Transportation History Collection, University of Michigan Library (Special Collections Research Center). BELOW RIGHT: Sycamore at Russell, 1967. Photo courtesy City of Davis and Bob Sommer.

## HOW DID WE GET HERE?

Dirt, paved, brick, cobblestone, concrete or asphalt, the street as a public right-of-way has served humans for thousands of years. Pedestrians, horses and horse-drawn carts shared the road for centuries, along with the occasional chicken, cow and goat.

The bicycle joined the street in the second decade of the 1800s, with the first bike path in America opening in 1894, running along the Ocean Parkway in Brooklyn. As bicycles became safer and cheaper and more women had access to the personal freedom bicycles provided, the bicycle came to symbolize the New Woman of the late 19th century, especially in Britain and the United States.[1] The first U.S. on-street dedicated bike lanes opened in Davis, California, in 1967, which led to similar bike facilities nationwide. Today, bikes outnumber cars worldwide by two to one.[2]

Those new-fangled motorized vehicles first hit the streets in 1886. Initially their numbers grew slowly and, in fact, some thought they would never amount to much: "There will never be a mass market for motor cars—about 1,000 in Europe—because that is the limit on the number of chauffeurs available!"[3] That threshold was blown past in 1908 when America fell in love with the Ford Model T, the first car for the masses. The love affair lasted for a hundred years. Cars became a symbol of freedom— freedom to go wherever we want, whenever we want. And our streets have accommodated this.

Construction of a national roadway network—starting with the Lincoln Highway in 1913, the early national highway system in the 1920s and the more comprehensive Interstate Highway System in the 1950s—led to unprecedented growth in private transportation and mobility and greatly contributed to the nation's economic output. It made the automobile the preferred mode of transportation for most Americans and signaled the end of the railroads as the predominant method of transportation for people. Passenger transportation is now dominated by private passenger vehicles (cars, trucks, vans and motorcycles), which account for 86 percent of passenger-miles traveled.[4] The automobile took over the road and overwhelmed other uses of the street. Street designs in the U.S. were based on the turning radius of fire trucks; the main goal was to keep vehicular traffic flowing. Streets became conflict zones between cars, bicyclists and pedestrians.

### WHERE ARE WE?

The typical American car is parked 95 percent of the time.[5] Yet our roadways and parking systems are designed to ensure fast travels for the two hours of peak car use a day: getting to work in the morning and getting home in the evening. The results are often overbuilt streets that take tremendous amounts of public space, yet often don't help people successfully navigate through them. Today the vast amount of land devoted to roads—more than 4 million miles of paved and unpaved roads—is more than the land for either parks or government buildings.[6] It's roughly one-third of all city lands.[7]

The large amount of land devoted to our roads has not actually provided the desired mobility benefits. The 2010 Annual Urban Mobility Report found that traffic congestion cost the U.S. almost $115 billion in 2009. This cost the average commuter more than $800 and about 34 hours per year.[8] And, unfortunately, the decades-long focus on vehicular mobility at the expense of safety and non-motorized users of the streets has resulted in unsafe and unfriendly pedestrian and bicycle environments.

The majority of pedestrian and bicyclist fatalities share a common thread: they occurred along "arterial" roadways that were dangerous by design; streets engineered for speeding traffic often with little or no provision for people on foot, in wheelchairs or on bicycles.[9, 10] Between

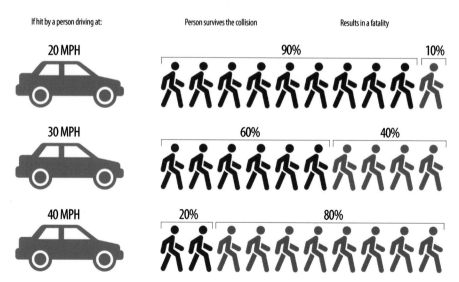

| If hit by a person driving at: | Person survives the collision | Results in a fatality |
| --- | --- | --- |
| 20 MPH | 90% | 10% |
| 30 MPH | 60% | 40% |
| 40 MPH | 20% | 80% |

LEFT: Diagram by Anne Fritzler/San Francisco Municipal Transportation Agency.

2010 and 2015 pedestrian deaths increased dramatically. But more cities are now embracing the concept that it is simply not acceptable for so many people to die or be injured on our streets. It has to stop.

Many cities and towns have begun to reverse this trend by better addressing the needs of pedestrians and bicyclists, building on the principles of the Complete Streets and Livable Streets movements. In New York alone, from 2006 to 2010, more than 250 miles of dedicated bicycle lanes were created and several laws to promote cycling were passed.[11] More than 700 cities in 50 countries now have bike-share programs; that number is increasing exponentially.

Many approaches to travel way design in America, such as multi-way boulevards and corridors with roundabouts, have successfully maintained or increased the roadway capacity for automobiles, while allowing streets to provide safer and more welcoming environments to pedestrians, cyclists and transit users. And jurisdictions are retrofitting sidewalks and crosswalks with ADA-compliant ramps and cross slopes and cues such as truncated domes.

Streets designed for bicyclists and pedestrians show a clear improvement in overall safety of street users and a dramatic decrease in accidents and injuries. More and more agencies are realizing that retrofitting existing roads to accommodate non-automobile users need not be viewed as a "zero sum game." Virtually always,

ABOVE RIGHT: San Francisco Vision Zero Campaign design and photo by MIG, Inc. BELOW RIGHT: South 11th Avenue, Bozeman, Montana. Photo: Catherine Courtenaye/MIG,Inc.

INTRODUCTION

7

better mobility for pedestrians and bicyclists can be added *without* diminishing the mobility of motorists. And, pedestrian and bicycle infrastructure construction projects also create more jobs than road construction jobs.[12] There's simply no need for warfare between modes of travel.

With the Complete Streets movement, many roadway designs are more sensitive to surrounding land uses and to the needs of bicyclists and pedestrians, supporting walkable and bikeable communities, compact development and mixed land use.[13] But the objectives for streets remained the same: move things around. Now, the Complete Streets concepts can be the basis of an even more ambitious transformation of streets to come.

### WHERE ARE WE GOING?

We're going places with different ideas about the cars we're driving—or not driving. The current Baby Boomer cohort of retirees is the first in which almost everyone has driven; more than 90 percent of Americans aged 60–64 drive. But those older drivers are now driving less. Younger drivers are getting their licenses later and they're not necessarily traveling in cars they own. People of all ages are making more virtual trips via online buying, telecommuting and social media. And with 77 percent of Millennials living in urban areas (up from 69 percent of Generation Xers when they were that age), they don't need to drive as much or as far.[14]

Millennials have entered adulthood with no memory of cheap gas and affordable car insurance. In a 2014 survey, 64 percent of Millennials surveyed said they don't want a car because it's too expensive.[15] They also have a different ownership model, comfortable with on-demand services and peer-to-peer sharing rather than owning content or devices. Layer on car share, bike-share and ride-share services, and real-time arrivals apps for public transit, and they find little reason to own a car. In the same survey, 81 percent said they use shared services because they have the same advantages of owning a car or bike, without the inconvenience and cost. And their attitudes about public transit are different from Baby Boomers. People aged 16 to 34, with jobs in households with incomes over $70,000—clearly not transit-dependent— increased their public transit use by 100 percent between 2000 and 2009.

That doesn't mean there won't be more cars; cars sales usually spike whenever gas prices drop. But, at least in western world urban areas, those cars are just parked more than ever. The International Transport Forum predicts that by 2050—if the *developing* world follows the historic consumption patterns of richer cities—the total number of cars could triple. Which makes reconsidering streets even *more* important for them.

### ARE WE THERE YET?

The future of transportation—and our streets—is already here. There will likely be fewer cars in most

RIGHT: Bell Street, Seattle. Project design and photo by MIG, Inc.

9

INTRODUCTION

major urban cities as we change to more of a shared car model. And they will be different because digital technology has changed everything.

Semiautonomous cars have been on the road with cameras, radar and ultrasonic systems that can see the world around. In fact, fully autonomous driverless electric cars are on the road too, opening up new possibilities for those with impaired vision to "drive" themselves anywhere they want to go (photo on facing page). Companies like GM are developing fleets of robot taxis to hit the roads, promising "zero crashes, zero emissions and zero congestion."[16] Many car engineers predict that cars and transportation will change more in the next 20 years than they have in the past 75 years.[17, 18] In 2017, Silicon Valley-based electric car company Tesla, Inc., passed iconic Ford Motor Company in market value—a company exactly 100 years older. The market clearly sees the future.

Communications systems and sensors installed in both streets and cars will create intelligent roads, keeping track of vehicles and the infrastructure around them. The Federal Communications Commission has already reserved a radio spectrum for communications among cars and between cars and infrastructure. Driving apps can monitor a car's braking and acceleration times, then share the information to create real-time congestion maps. And cars wouldn't crash with each other, or with bicyclists and pedestrians. Cars could then be made of lighter materials and could pack closer together,

traveling in platoons to reduce congestion—and opening areas of streets for other uses.

Mandating new technologies for safety is not new. Seatbelts, airbag, anti-lock brakes and stabilization systems are now required. Cars with anti-collision and traffic-calming technologies are becoming the norm, as will autonomous cars. And when commuters are able to work, chat, check emails and even sleep in cars as they currently do on trains and many buses, a commute will be part of a work day or the evening's entertainment.

## HOW MUCH LONGER?

America built about 40,000 miles of interstate highways to get the country moving after World War II. During the 1990s, when gas was cheap, the economy booming and driving increasing, the nation built about 17,000 lane-miles a year. From 2005 to 2013, the nation built 317,000 lane-miles of new roads—about 40,000 miles every year.[19] Road construction continues as if demand will always be increasing. And it costs a lot of money. States and the federal government spend about $27 billion a year on road expansion, spread pretty evenly between highways and surface streets. Not road maintenance. Road expansion.

That's the fatal flaw in America's transportation infrastructure policy: It's still vehicle-oriented planning. Much of transportation planning is based on policies, design manuals and ways of thinking of the 1990s.

INTRODUCTION

*11*

We're building more and more roads and parking with the aim of shaving a few seconds off of a half-hour commute. And we're not investing at the same pace in transit, maintenance, and ensuring a multimodal mobility balance on our streets.

It's time to be bold.

### WE ARE THERE

Let's reconsider how streets can expand the public realm and provide real social and economic benefits to all our communities and neighborhoods.

We now have the tools to incorporate uncertainty into transportation planning. Transportation investment decisions can reflect that driving will decline in the developed world. The changed driving habits among younger generations must be factored into community and transportation planning, starting now, to ensure that transportation investments serve the needs and desires of communities today and in the decades to come. And the developing world can learn from the historic prioritization of cars—and build it better.

The very nature of streets can change. Streets *are* the public realm. By designing for what might be coming in the future—driverless cars, big data traffic operations, no cars at all—cities can create streets that change to meet changing needs. They can become true public space, with social gathering, events, play, commerce and urban agriculture and green space—all of the potential street functions covered in the next chapters.

This book examines how streets can function in many different ways and still provide mobility for moving goods and people. It explores how street innovations such as various types of traffic calming, flexible street design, slow zones, narrower lanes, fewer road markings and signage and more shared space will expand the function of streets—because they are for living, not just driving.

INTRODUCTION

## GET THE MOST FROM THIS BOOK

We've designed this book to offer ideas and concepts about how we're reconsidering streets and the public realm. But it's also a workbook, with case studies and best practices from around the world—advice from the trenches of successful street transformations.

We begin with "Street Design Principles," a set of things to keep in mind while considering a street redesign.

We then grouped types of activities streets can support into six chapters: mobility and wayfinding (move), social streets (gather), play streets (play), shopping streets (shop), farm streets (grow) and resilient streets (green).

Within each chapter you will find:

**An activities burst.** We started our thinking with the basic types of activities people might do on a street (see facing page). In each chapter we suggest both the activities you might find on that specific type of street (for example, a play street or a shopping street), and some activities from another type of street that might also be appropriate on that street.

**Case studies.** We go into great analytical depth for at least two example streets per chapter, providing photos and measured plans and elevation schematics so you can see precisely how the street works. We also provide many short case studies and references. Case studies are a snapshot in time—communities change, technology changes and a street might be redesigned again. But that's the point of this book: flexible streets can respond to future opportunities.

**Physical elements.** Introducing specific physical elements on a street induces behavior change in people, encouraging them to interact, socialize or play. While there are necessary elements that are common to all streets, we also provide examples of elements to consider specific to each type of street.

**Best practices.** Based on all the case studies and our own work designing streets, we developed best practices, with photos and illustrations, to help you plan and design your own great streets.

**Before and after photo simulation.** And last, a snapshot of a real street undergoing a transformation.

You might just want to zip through, reading from cover to cover. We also encourage you to spend some time with each street, getting to know it and how you might apply its best practices to your own streets.

**MOVE**
Biking · Riding · Driving · Walking · Servicing · Strolling · Navigating · Rolling/skating · Locating · Parking · Interpreting · Running · Orienting

**GATHER**
Demonstrating · People watching · Networking · Teaching · Resting · Learning · Parading · Eating · Talking · Sitting · Playing music · Meeting · Singing · Dancing

**SHOP**
Dining · Manufacturing · Producing · Cooking · Browsing · Buying · Displaying · Bartering · Performing · Bargaining · Selling

**PLAY**
Sensing · Sliding · Thinking · Jumping · Geocaching · Drawing · Exercising · Reading · Building · Discovering · Balancing · Playing games · Climbing

**GROW**
Irrigating · Mulching · Planting · Weeding · Propagating · Pruning · Composting · Harvesting · Storing

**GREEN**
Managing waste · Harvesting water · Reusing · Recycling · Rejuvenating · Creating habitat · Generating energy · Distributing materials · Cleansing water

### ACTIVITIES ON THE STREET

"Design is not our end goal. Our end goal is to connect people to each other."[20] Great street design supports human behavior. We have grouped activities into six types of streets, but activities in different groups can occur on the same street. Not all activities can occur on every street, but flexible streets can incorporate a range of activities for people of all ages and abilities at different times of the day and for different days of the week. (Watch for this activities burst in each chapter.)

## 2

# STREET DESIGN PRINCIPLES

*Living Streets*

Many different types of streets serve different purposes, but all streets should be designed recognizing that *humans* will be using the street. Streets operate differently when designed for high volume, fast traffic or for slow moving, low volumes. People behave differently according to age, abilities, interests and family situation, at different times of day, day of the week or season of the year.

A well-designed grid of streets will provide the community with different experiences—both when traveling and when lingering. Here are some overarching principles to keep in mind while considering a street redesign, to help determine the appropriate expanded functions, elements and programming for a range of streets.

## BASIC STREET PRINCIPLES

When embarking on a street redesign, consider these five guiding principles and the design principles that follow:

**Design for Humans.** Most of our streets are too large, too wide (often wide enough to land a passenger plane) and monotonously long, with little detail to engage the human eye. They lack the intimate feel that allows users, especially pedestrians and bicyclists, to feel safe and comfortable. Street corridors don't need to have any more than 50 percent of the space devoted to cars, and all excess space not used by cars can then be repurposed. Reducing street width, breaking up the length, and adding medians, trees, art and vertical elements can create a series of interconnected living rooms with a beginning, middle and an end.

**Right Size.** If travel lanes are too wide, they encourage speeding. If bike facilities are too wide and unprotected, they encourage vehicles to use them as an additional lane, or just drive faster. If sidewalks are too wide and not activated by adjoining ground floor uses, they feel stark and uninviting. Ensuring that travel lanes, bike facilities, pedestrian pathways and crosswalks are appropriately sized in relation to each other creates mutual respect between the different modes of travel.

**Provide Multiple Benefits.** Especially in today's economic climate, it's important to maximize impact by designing and locating streetscape elements that offer multiple benefits.

RIGHT AND PRECEDING PAGE: Tower of the Americas Way, San Antonio.

Project design and photo by MIG, Inc.

For example, a tree provides shade, helps clean the air, and can be positioned to calm traffic. Lighting illuminates an area, while also providing a feeling of enclosure, safety and a sense of identity for the area. And sidewalks provide areas for pedestrians to walk and stroll, while allowing opportunities for outdoor dining and other commercial activities. These are critical economic development opportunities for small and large businesses, and can provide a valuable source of income for towns and cities.

**Design for multimodal shift.** Ensuring that walking, biking and taking transit feels safe, convenient and comfortable is the basic foundation for shifting short and medium trips away from cars. Envisioning walking, biking and transit as the primary modes of travel is a paradigm shift in how we design streets.

**Design for Tomorrow.** Technology is constantly evolving, as are the sizes and types of vehicles we drive. Technological advancements in traffic signalization have already increased the overall capacity of roads, as will driverless technology. So design streets to ensure that streetscape improvements like redesigned curbs don't impede future opportunities. For example, flexible sidewalks can be designed at the same grade as rest of the street, with bollards and planter boxes providing the same sense of safety as concrete curbs. As travel lanes for cars decrease in size, the extra space created can be used for wider sidewalks, more trees, and more bicycle and pedestrian amenities.

LEFT: First Street, Long Beach, California.
Project design and photo by MIG, Inc.

# ❶ Aesthetically Pleasing

Human beings are naturally sensitive to the physical world and respond to beauty. Street benches don't need to be hard, flat plastic. Wood, art, trees, lights and details attract the eye and humanize the environment. Color, textures, natural elements, sounds, smells and level of detail should work together to engage people and invite them in.

RIGHT: City of Funchal, Madeira, Portugal.

Photo by Anton Zelenov/Shutterstock.com

**2**

# Connectivity

Streets are one part of a larger jigsaw puzzle; what happens on one street affects other streets around it. Some streets clearly need to function as arterials that keep cars moving; others can focus more on pedestrian and bicyclist shared space. Block sizes of 200 feet by 200 feet make Downtown Portland a most walkable grid. A well-connected grid encourages people to walk and bike; the more intersections and crossing points, the more pedestrian-friendly the street is. The grid also slows cars, giving the occupants time to view what's available on the street and maybe decide to stop and walk too.

LEFT: Downtown Portland.
Photo by Google Earth.

**21**

### ❸
# Safety

Safety includes both avoiding conflicts between travel modes and personal security to increase comfort level. The physical design of a street should be safe enough that, for example, parents don't feel they must cling to a child's hand at all times. That may require a buffer from quickly moving traffic or increasing the width of a pedestrian-only zone. Surfaces should be maintained to reduce tripping and there should not be any places for people to hide. Adjoining uses are also important. Buildings with windows instead of blank walls increase eyes on the street and provide a perceived sense of safety. Finally, streets should be well lit to be safe at all times of day.

RIGHT: Main Street, Lyons, Colorado.

Project design and photo by MIG, Inc.

④
# Universal Accessibility

Streets should ensure that people of all abilities—using canes, wheelchairs, dogs and assistive devices—and using all modes of travel can use them, including skateboards, roller blades, tricycles and strollers. There should be different types of cues for people with low vision, people in wheelchairs and those with difficulty hearing. The elderly may need more places to sit along the street; bladers and bicyclists may need their own lane.

LEFT: West Capitol Avenue, West Sacramento.

Project design and photo by MIG, Inc.

**⑤**

# Context Sensitivity: Climate

Streets should feel like places of respite, especially during hot summer months when trees can provide shade. In areas that get very hot, street trees can provide shade. For example, Sacramento's and Savannah's urban forests reduce downtown temperatures by four degrees.

In cold climates, deciduous trees can also become part of lighting and decorations.

ABOVE: Jones Street and Bull Street, Savannah, Georgia.

Photo by Ken Lund. Licensed under Creative Commons 2.0.

RIGHT: Trondheim, Norway.

Photo by Lee Dyer. "The beautiful night streets of Trondheim at Christmas4." Licensed under Creative Commons 2.0.

## ❻ Context Sensitivity: Ecosystems and Resilience

Streets have the potential to mitigate increasing flooding issues, become sanctuaries during disasters and increase a city's resilience. They also affect their surrounding local and regional environment. The type of landscaping and plant palette should be appropriate for that area. If the street drains into a stormwater inlet or nearby river, water runoff should be cleansed onsite before it flows into pipes and/or into a body of water. The street's connection to surrounding hills and open spaces should also be taken into account.

LEFT: Vine Street, Seattle.
Project design and photo by MIG, Inc.

LIVING STREETS

25

⑦
# Context Sensitivity: Physical Surroundings

Streets should respond to their physical context—whether the main uses are commercial, industrial, institutional or residential—and to the needs of the people inside the buildings. Street design should connect the two sides of the street, so people walking on one side can relate to and easily cross over to the other side. Pedestrians don't respond well to very wide streets. That might mean, for example, reducing the width of travel lanes, converting travel lanes to bike paths and medians, adding bulb outs at corners, and ensuring that landscaping doesn't inhibit the visibility of retail frontages.

RIGHT: West Capitol Avenue, West Sacramento.

Project design and photo by MIG, Inc.

## 8
# Temporal Flexibility

Streets can operate differently on different occasions (time of day, day of week, season of the year). Sometimes parking lanes can be repurposed for a farmers market, sidewalks can provide space for commerce in the evenings, or the street can host a special event that requires it to be entirely closed. Design for flexibility.

FAR LEFT AND LEFT: Bell Street, Seattle.
Project design and photos by MIG, Inc.

LIVING STREETS

27

**9**
# Cultural Sensitivity

Streets serve local community needs, so the design and programming of the street should respond to those needs. Some communities like outdoor dining, music or street art. Others don't. Ask community members about their preferences to ensure the right mix of elements.

RIGHT: Nueva Street, San Antonio.
Project design and photo by MIG, Inc.

**10**

# Fun and Enjoyment

Let's have fun on the street! Allow people to enjoy the street, so it's not just a place for commuting. Design can allow spaces for people to gather, and programming such as music, dances and exercising. And even just busking can provide the impetus for social gathering on the street.

LEFT: Beech Croft Road, Oxford, England.

Photo by Ted Dewan. Licensed under Creative Commons 2.0.

BELOW: Sidewalk band.

Photo by Peter. "Band, France." Licensed under Creative Commons 2.0.

# 11
# Diversity of behavior

Streetscapes should offer multiple opportunities for different modes of behavior including socializing, eating, meeting friends, conducting commerce, or just being alone. Adaptable, flexible streets can respond to changing human needs.

RIGHT: Bell Street, Seattle.
Project design and photo by MIG, Inc.

# Emergency Access and Maintenance

Successful street design allows for emergency access and ease of operations (such as snow removal and storage), as well as needed repairs to utilities above and below the street (stormwater, sewage, water, electric, phone, gas and cable). Streets must also accommodate garbage pick-up and recycling, and ensure access for police, fire and medical personnel and other first responders.

LEFT: 13th Street and U Street, NW, Washington D.C.

Photo by Elvert Barnes. "01.MenWork.13U. NW.WDC.17April2013." Licensed under Creative Commons 2.0.

31

## ⑬ Community Building

Improvements to the design of a street should accommodate all the activities and special events that historically have taken place there. People need to feel comfortable that they'll be able to continue to live and work on that street. A gritty street retains its grittiness. Ideally, opportunities for small-scale "mom and pop" stores should remain and not be displaced by new streetscape improvements. The street can be inclusive of current users while attracting new people to use and enjoy the street.

RIGHT: Pogo Park #1 (Elm Playlot),
Elm Avenue and 8th Street,
Richmond, California.

Photo by Maria Durana.

## ⑭ Community Ownership

Involving the community in street design is essential. The street should tell the story of the people who live and work along it, the culture, history and geography of the area. That reinforces community members' connection to each other, fosters a sense of pride in their neighborhood and encourages the community to help maintain the street—whether that's simply picking up a piece of trash, volunteering to maintain a street garden or helping to install improvements.

LEFT: 31st Avenue, Queens, New York.

Photo by Costa Constantinides. Licensed under Creative Commons 2.0.

LIVING STREETS

**33**

## 3

### MOVE ALONG THE STREET

*Flexible Streets*

We're stuck. Not in traffic, although we are sometimes that too. We're stuck in how we think about mobility and finding our way on the street. But a fresh combination of physical design, technology and programming can result in streets for all types of uses, engaging all our senses at all times of the day.

Slowing traffic and eliminating curbs: those two design interventions can shorten travel times for vehicles, increase and enhance mobility for bicyclists and pedestrians, increase commerce, and allow for many other opportunities on the street, including shared social space.

SMITH ST.

The way we build roads affects more than just the movement of vehicles. Street design determines how drivers behave on the street, whether pedestrians feel safe to walk and linger, and what kinds of businesses and housing are built along its edges.

One of the first steps in rethinking a street is determining its current functional classification and whether it's correct for the surrounding community, as well as for mobility and wayfinding. Cities and towns contain many different types of streets with different levels of traffic volume, speed and types of users. Traditional street classification systems prioritized vehicular traffic over other modes and defined just three types of streets: High-speed, high-volume arterial roads; low-speed local streets; and the connectors between them.[1]

Many cities are adding even more classifications that reflect their own communities, such as local streets with very low speeds and very pedestrian-friendly main streets. Concentrating on the *human* element—because for the moment humans are still driving the vehicles and bicycles and doing the walking—shifts the paradigm.

## NAVIGATING THE STREET
Successful street mobility and navigation depend on the legibility of the urban fabric and the clarity of its spatial features. In his book *Image of the City,* Kevin Lynch defines:

**Paths:** Channels by which people move, such as streets and sidewalks.

**Edges:** All the other lines not included in paths such as walls, sides of buildings and linear open spaces.

**Nodes:** Points or places where there is a concentration of activity or a major focus or feature such as a landscaped garden, busy corner or a city center.

**Landmarks:** Physical elements that act as reference points and help with orientation such as a notable building, a hill, a roundabout or a well-known retail establishment.

**Districts:** Sections of the City that have a specific identity.

The ability of drivers, bicyclists and pedestrians to navigate successfully through and between those organizing features depends on how easy it is to understand and interpret the myriad number of cues received from the street. We perceive those cues through our physical senses, transmit this sensory data to processing centers in the brain, and then respond and take action.

Dutch traffic engineer Hans Monderman said: "A wide road with a lot of street signs is telling a story. It's saying, go ahead, don't worry, go as fast as you want, there's no need to pay attention to your surroundings. And that's a very dangerous message."[2]

Over half of the brain is devoted to vision; we rely primarily on sight to perceive the world around us.[3] But, the immense amount of visual information available to us is overwhelming. Consequently, we adapt to this onslaught by limiting what we take in. For example, when driving down a street, a driver will scan the available paths, signage and markings, glancing at specific points for less than two-tenths of a second before moving on to the next point.[4] The more separate pieces of information a driver sees and needs to process, the less legible the street becomes and the longer it takes to find and act on the information that's needed to navigate successfully.

People don't simply need *more* information on the street to help them navigate. They need information that is tied to more senses or, sometimes, they need no information at all. Traditional traffic-calming measures add physical elements like bulb outs or speed bumps, but they still "communicate" that pavement is for cars and sidewalks are for pedestrians, making signs and other markings a necessity for telling people what to do.

By removing signage and artificial barriers such as curbs, lines and sidewalks, we force drivers to rely on their own perceptions of the street. "Psychological traffic calming" relies on social and cultural norms rather than signs and markings to moderate human behavior. For example, adding irregular vertical elements such as trees or visually complex material such as flowerbeds or café tables close to the street sends cues that this is a place for people and pedestrians. Interrupting sight lines to shorten the view adds uncertainty about what's ahead, making drivers more careful. And eliminating sidewalks, making them flush with the street with different pavement treatments, blurs the line between vehicle and pedestrian space, signaling drivers to slow down.

Taking it one step further, some streets have no traditional traffic control elements at all: no signals, crosswalks or other markings. These are the "naked streets" Monderman espouses.

In Wiltshire, England, removing the centerline on some streets reduced average speeds from over 40 mph to less than 30 mph, which reduced injury collisions by 35 percent.[5] Streets are then not just conduits for vehicles; drivers must negotiate street space on an equal footing with pedestrians and bicyclists.

Similarly, conventional wayfinding includes physical signage and sometimes the sense of touch. But before modern wayfinding elements and signage, the historic cores of towns and cities relied less on signs and more on multiple senses—smell, touch, sounds and even taste— to advertise key destinations and shops. These cities and towns created unique, multisensory experiences, offering different sensory experiences on different streets, at different times of the day.[6]

Today's environmental design experts acknowledge the advantages of using multisensory wayfinding to interpret layered information tied to a place that can't be discovered relying solely on vision.[7] Streets can build on recent concepts in conventional wayfinding, incorporate new technology and blend in all five senses to enhance wayfinding and navigation, improving our overall street experience.

## WHY CHANGE THE STREET?

Infrastructure doesn't need to be built with massive amounts of concrete that will last 100 years. Paint and other temporary design elements can be more effective and far cheaper than pouring concrete. Streets don't need to have permanent speed limits; dynamic traffic controls and programmable speed signs allow speeds to change to improve traffic flow as needed. Travel lanes and parking lanes don't need to be permanently assigned; smart studs, indicator lights, temporary bollards and travel gates can change lane uses and even travel direction during the day or on different days of the week. Parking policies don't have to disrupt the urban fabric; limits on parking can actually increase commerce.[8] Bicycles don't have to be squeezed and forced to dodge car doors; narrowing vehicle travel lanes through restriping creates more space for bicycles. And pedestrians don't have to be relegated to the sidewalk only; shared space can help all users navigate.

Not all streets are suitable for all uses. Parkways, expressways and highways are clearly devoted to fast-moving vehicular traffic. But main streets, local streets, and even boulevards and avenues can be flexible, functioning differently at different times of day or on different days of the week, providing many more community benefits.

## GOALS

Each street plays a role with a distinct purpose and function within the larger roadway network, and the design goals for that street are determined accordingly. The goals of flexible streets are to:

• Encourage all types of users, of all ages and abilities.
• Create opportunities for streets to be used at all times of day and days of the week.
• Provide shared space for people to use.

**MOVE**

Biking · Riding · Driving · Walking · Servicing · Strolling · Navigating · Rolling/skating · Locating · Parking · Interpreting · Running · Orienting

**GATHER**

Demonstrating · People watching · Networking · Teaching · Resting · Learning · Parading · Eating · Talking · Sitting · Playing music · Meeting · Singing · Dancing

**SHOP**

Dining · Manufacturing · Producing · Cooking · Browsing · Buying · Displaying · Bartering · Performing · Bargaining · Selling

**PLAY**

Sensing · Sliding · Thinking · Jumping · Geocaching · Drawing · Exercising · Reading · Building · Discovering · Balancing · Playing games · Climbing

**GROW**

Irrigating · Mulching · Planting · Weeding · Propagating · Pruning · Composting · Harvesting · Storing

**GREEN**

Managing waste · Harvesting water · Rejuvenating · Parking · Reusing · Recycling · Creating habitat · Generating energy · Distributing materials · Cleansing water

### ACTIVITIES ON THE FLEXIBLE STREET

Mobility and wayfinding are primary functions of all streets. But many other activities can be accommodated as well. When incorporating activities, such as play or commerce, the three main aspects of mobility—walking, biking and driving—must always be taken into account.

## OCTAVIA BOULEVARD
*San Francisco, California*

What was once an elevated freeway cutting through swaths of blighted areas is now a pedestrian-friendly, tree-lined boulevard that has revitalized the mainly residential Hayes Valley neighborhood. Portions of the Central Freeway, built in the 1950s, were irreparably damaged during the massive 1989 Loma Prieta earthquake. Consequently, the community voted to take down the entire freeway. Rather than build a traditional four- or six-lane highway, the City selected a boulevard design. Octavia Boulevard now has two median-divided lanes of through traffic that are separated by a generous landscaped buffer from two one-lane frontage roads serving local

residents and on-street parking.[9] The speed limit for the central lanes is 30 miles per hour and 15 on the frontage roads.

The five intersections along the boulevard are controlled by traffic signals, while the frontage lanes are controlled by either stop signs or red flashing lights at the two heavy traffic intersections. All the lanes are allowed to turn in all directions at intersections so there are a number of potentially conflicting movements such as vehicles turning right from the central lane across straight-moving traffic on the side road. But, traffic studies have shown that central lane drivers do look right to yield to

RIGHT: Octavia Boulevard, San Francisco. Photo by Catherine Courtenaye/MIG, Inc.

FLEXIBLE STREETS

43

| 12' | 8' | 10' | 9' | 11' | 11' | 10' | 11' | 11' | 9' | 10' | 8' | 12' | Vacant Parcel |
|-----|----|----|----|----|----|----|----|----|----|----|----|----|----|
| Sidewalk | Parking | Travel Lane | Median | Travel Lane | Travel Lane | Median | Turn Lane | Travel Lane | Median | Travel Lane | Parking | Sidewalk | |

0'  2'  5'       15'

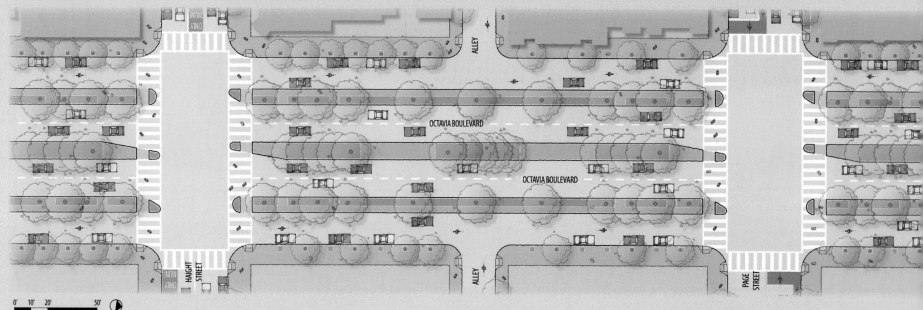

0'  10'  20'     50'

pedestrians, and thus also yield to frontage road drivers. Frontage road drivers, who have a stop sign even when the light is green, do look left to see if cars are coming.

There were initial concerns about traffic congestion, but the boulevard distributes traffic smoothly through the surrounding neighborhood, while maintaining links to the arterials served by the old freeway. A new park at the northern end adds tree-lined pedestrian walkways and more green space. Parcels freed up by freeway demolition were redeveloped into almost 1,000 units of badly needed housing. Commercial establishments changed from liquor stores and auto mechanics to restaurants and shops. And, without the bisecting freeway, the Hayes Valley neighborhood has greatly enhanced the quality of its public realm and has become more livable.[10]

**What Works**    More sidewalks and medians increase pedestrian and bicycle safety, while the at-grade design creates more eyes on the boulevard. • Decreased traffic volume improves air quality. • Sales of excess freeway right-of-way land generated money for public realm improvements. • Streetscape improvements increased real estate values and spurred economic development.

**Lessons Learned**    The northbound side road had five times the traffic as southbound so speed humps were added; traffic volume went down by 50% and median speed by almost 25%. • At 18.5 feet, frontage roads are wider than the often recommended 15 feet, which can increase speeds. • Boulevards work best on low-volume streets. • Peak-hour congestion can spill over onto surrounding streets.

# HEMISFAIR STREETS
*San Antonio, Texas*

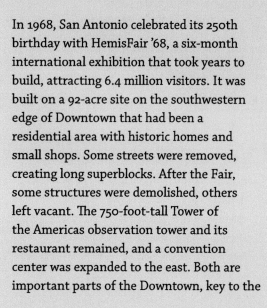

In 1968, San Antonio celebrated its 250th birthday with HemisFair '68, a six-month international exhibition that took years to build, attracting 6.4 million visitors. It was built on a 92-acre site on the southwestern edge of Downtown that had been a residential area with historic homes and small shops. Some streets were removed, creating long superblocks. After the Fair, some structures were demolished, others left vacant. The 750-foot-tall Tower of the Americas observation tower and its restaurant remained, and a convention center was expanded to the east. Both are important parts of the Downtown, key to the

City's economy. The old fairgrounds area was ostensibly a park, but 80 percent of it was paved. And in the 1980s, the new I-37 freeway provided faster, higher traffic flows down to the coast, but its many on/off ramps divided this area of Downtown in two. Economic activity declined.

In 2010, the community decided to "heal" the broken street grid. They demolished the original, aging convention center's western side—freeing up that area for a real park— and expanded it by a similar amount on the east side of the convention center. But the land on the east side was crisscrossed

RIGHT: Nueva Street, San Antonio. Project design and photo by MIG, Inc.

FLEXIBLE STREETS

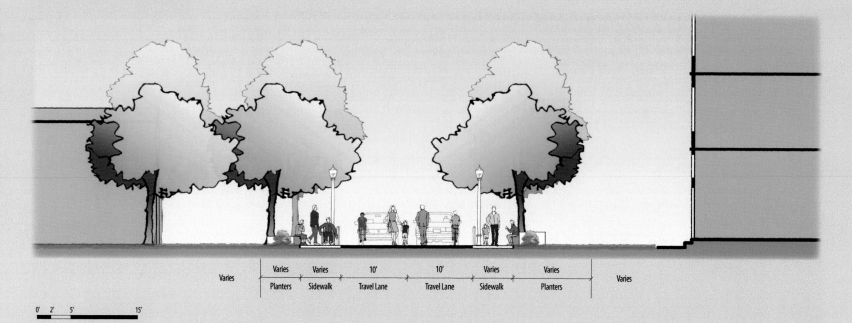

Varies

Varies | Varies | 10' | 10' | Varies | Varies

Planters | Sidewalk | Travel Lane | Travel Lane | Sidewalk | Planters

Varies

0'  2'  5'        15'

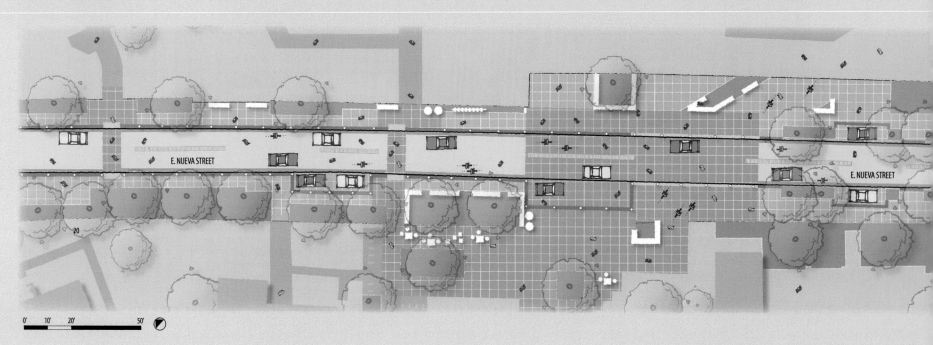

E. NUEVA STREET

20

E. NUEVA STREET

0'  10'  20'        50'

by three freeway on-ramps to I-37 and two streets that allowed traffic to flow at 50 miles per hour, with lots of unused, barren land in between.

The solution was to consolidate the on-ramps, reduce Tower of the Americas Way from four lanes to three lanes, reduce the width of the lanes from 14 feet to 11 feet and reduce the speed to 35 miles per hour. That change created room for large sidewalks and a two-way bike lane on the west side of the road. That change consolidated the travel lanes and left a large open space for a $400,000,000 expansion of the convention center and a new hotel. Three times as much parkland was created to the west and south, and bicycle and pedestrian connections were made to and through the park, to the River Walk, and to a neighborhood on the east side that had been cut off by the freeway. The project also brought back two streets that had existed before the superblocks, Nueva Way and Water Street. They are now very pedestrian-, bicycle- and wheelchair-friendly shared streets, enhancing connectivity and humanizing the entire area.

It may take cars an extra few seconds to access I-37, but the community agrees this is a small price to pay for all the benefits.[11]

RIGHT: Tower of the Americas Way, San Antonio. Project design and photo by MIG, Inc.

**What Works**   Creates a shared, mixed-use street in narrow right-of-way. • It's a true flexible street that is easily transformed into a festival street or other temporary uses. • Diverse materials such as plantings and large canopy trees slow down traffic. • It successfully attracted new development. • Stormwater planters improve water quality before it flows into the San Antonio River.

**Lessons Learned**   Greater education is needed about how low-water landscaping can create a beautiful and unique identity. • New landscaping should take into account traditional maintenance methods; there will be a learning curve and additional training may be needed. • Bike facilities may be underused until the entire bike network is built.

> FLEXIBLE STREETS

49

# BELL STREET

*Seattle, Washington*

It's a street....It's a park....It's a street that redefines a park.

Booming Seattle's high land prices meant it wasn't possible to acquire land for a new park in Belltown, the densest urban area of the City. But the area was increasing in population and a new community gathering space was very much needed. At the same time, Bell Street was underutilized and really due for upgrading.

The community worked with the City's Parks and Recreation Department to develop a vision. The solution was transforming a four-block street section of a single-purpose right-of-way into a vibrant, safe and green multifunctional public space. Bell Street Park is a hybrid of park activities and street functions—a park in a street. A subtle topographic shift raises the roadway up to the sidewalk level to create one continuous surface of shared space. Street and park materials are woven into a wall-to-wall tapestry of shared space with meandering paving, seating and lots of planting, forming a unified circuitry for the park space.

LEFT: Bell Street, Seattle. Project design and photo by MIG, Inc.

FLEXIBLE STREETS

51

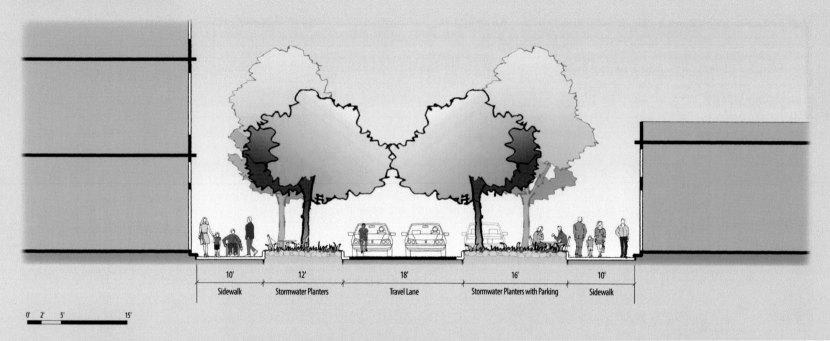

| 10' | 12' | 18' | 16' | 10' |
|---|---|---|---|---|
| Sidewalk | Stormwater Planters | Travel Lane | Stormwater Planters with Parking | Sidewalk |

0'  2'  5'                    15'

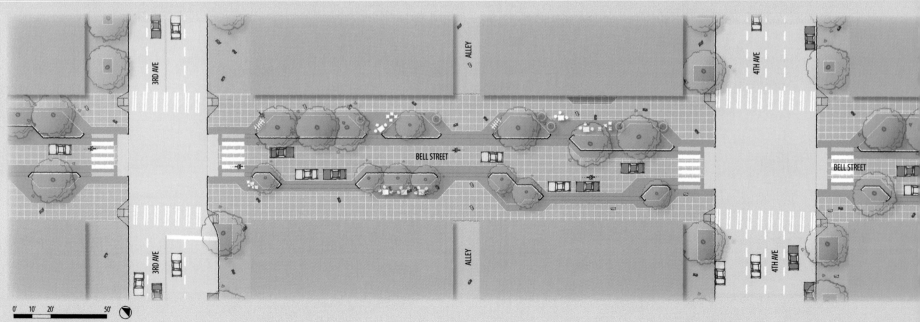

3RD AVE

ALLEY

4TH AVE

BELL STREET

BELL STREET

ALLEY

3RD AVE

4TH AVE

0'  10'  20'        50'

This portion of Bell Street is now an outdoor living room for residents, while still serving cars, buses, bicycles and emergency vehicles. On summer weekends, buses don't run on the street itself, creating shared space for vendors, music and dancing, other entertainment, art shows and markets, games, food, parades, yoga, planting and gardening parties, movies at night and general mingling and running around. The neighborhood now views the street as a true community amenity.

Completed in 2014 at a cost of $3 million, this four-block section is the first phase of a long-range plan for a park corridor stretching all the way from South Lake Union to Elliott Bay.

**What Works**    It is an innovative park street that creates usable open space in a built out downtown neighborhood. • It can easily become a temporary festival street. • The planting, design, use of materials combine to create a place with a unique identity. • It has attracted a huge amount of private investment on both sides of the street. • It is an inclusive place that provides opportunities for residents, workers and homeless to relax and enjoy the streetscape amenities.

**Lessons Learned**    There is an opportunity to slow down the traffic even more, which would allow it to become more of a shared street. • The street could benefit from more programming which would activate the street and lead to more use of its open space amenities.

## NOORDKADE
*Drachten, Netherlands*

Drachten is a 17-century town that has grown into a bustling city. One of its central streets, Noordkade, is a busy road that handles up to 20,000 cars a day, regional buses and thousands of bicyclists and pedestrians. It's also "naked."

In 2001 Dutch traffic engineer Hans Monderman looked at the unattractive streets and signal-controlled intersections and ripped out all the traditional elements used by traffic engineers to influence driver behavior: traffic lights, curbs, road markings and pedestrian crossings.

Monderman designed the street to change alignments as cars drive along it. Noordkade starts with an open space with trees, benches and plantings along each side of the open space. Cars drive next to the open space. Then the road switches so they drive in the middle of the road with parking along the side. Then vehicles are on the outside lanes, with a wide middle median for diagonal vehicle parking, bike parking, seating and trees. And sometimes the road runs along a canal. Most key intersections are roundabouts or squareabouts (a roundabout that's an integral part of a public square). A distinguishing feature of the roundabouts is

RIGHT: Noordkade and Torenstraat, Drachten, Netherlands. Photo by Raban Haaijk, courtesy *Works that Work*.

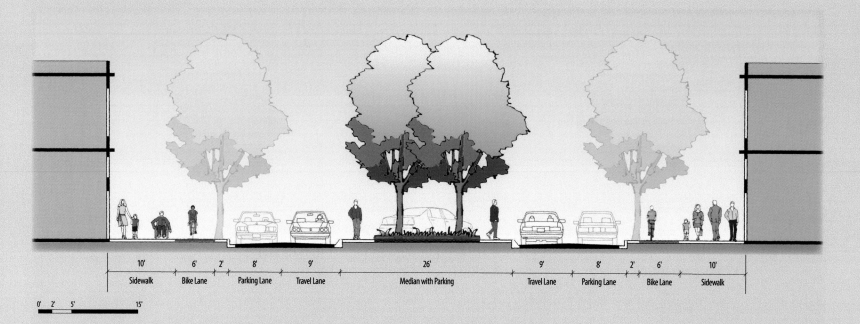

| 10' | 6' | 2' | 8' | 9' | 26' | 9' | 8' | 2' | 6' | 10' |
|-----|-----|-----|-----|-----|-----|-----|-----|-----|-----|-----|
| Sidewalk | Bike Lane | | Parking Lane | Travel Lane | Median with Parking | Travel Lane | Parking Lane | | Bike Lane | Sidewalk |

0'  2'  5'        15'

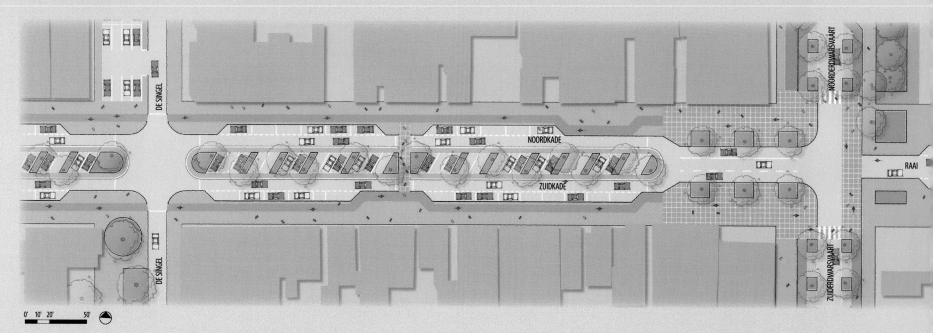

0'  10'  20'    50'

the lack of separation between cyclists and cars. The approach roads have bicycle lanes, but as soon as cyclists enter the roundabout they completely share the road with vehicles.

Drivers now see few signs or signals telling them how fast to go, who has right-of-way or just what they're supposed to do. They have only special paving to emphasize pedestrian zones and parking areas, and raised crosswalks. Since it's not immediately clear where the car zone ends and the pedestrian or bicycle zone begins, the shared environment causes drivers to slow down, usually to 20 mph or lower, a speed that provides enough time to figure out what other drivers, bicyclists and pedestrians are going to do. It's all done through eye contact and hand signals, with pedestrians, cyclists and other streets users deciding amongst themselves when it's safe to proceed. At speeds of 20 mph or below, the chance of being severely injured in a traffic crash is relatively low.

The salient feature of Noordkade is not its "nakedness" but that it is fully part of the public realm. Its legibility allows all types of users to understand that it is a shared environment, and the users behave accordingly.

**What Works** Wonderful use of design, changing every four blocks while still allowing for all modes of travel. • Integrates parking in innovative ways that don't detract from the landscaping design. • Individual shops and outdoor eating are very close to vehicle travel lanes, causing them to slow down. • Traffic crash rates have fallen by about 20 percent since the conversion, while travel time has improved.

**Lessons Learned** Additional pedestrian crossings were added later. • The approach cannot be applied to every street and intersection; the solution for each street depends on traffic volumes, intersection geometry, topography and the prevailing mix of uses. • Just as on marked streets, some people will break the "rules." • When crashes happen, it may be difficult to determine which party is at fault.

# VISION ZERO SF

*San Francisco, California*

Over 500 people were struck and severely injured by cars in San Francisco yearly, one of the worst records in the country. And in 2016, 30 people died. But in 2017, the number of fatalities dropped by one-third, to the lowest level in the City's history. The difference was Vision Zero, an ethics-based approach to traffic safety that started in Sweden. Conventional wisdom had been grounded in cost-benefit analysis, accepting that some traffic deaths are inevitable. Vision Zero maintains that deaths are unacceptable and preventable. It calls for investing in behavior change education, along with engineering (traffic calming,

signaling changes, pedestrian zones, etc.) and enforcement (warnings and tickets).

Some of the major human causes of crashes are obvious: Speeding and distracted driving such as texting and using apps. (Perhaps surprisingly, drunk driving is no longer the main cause.) But how to change those behaviors is not so obvious. A key change is to combat the "us vs. them" narrative (cars versus motorcycles, bicyclists and pedestrians) by shifting people's thinking away from traffic safety as a personal responsibility and towards a collective responsibility frame that acknowledges the

LEFT: Project design and photos by MIG, Inc.

FLEXIBLE STREETS

LOWER LEFT: San Francisco analyzed pedestrian/bicyclist-involved car crashes to determine on which streets the combination of education, engineering and enforcement would be most effective.

LEFT: Project design and photos by MIG, Inc.

role of the built environment and policy decisions—as well as our own actions.

The education campaigns targeted specific audiences (e.g., males age 18–48 who are more likely to speed). The Vision Zero SF message framework recognized that everyone has different levels of awareness. The messaging flows through stages—from no knowledge to becoming an advocate for safer streets:

1. Developing an awareness that there is a problem. (My son died at this intersection)

2. Developing an understanding of the problem. (We share these streets, we can make them safer)

3. Developing an understanding of solutions and then actively participating in solutions. (Distracted Driving is Deadly Driving; It Stops Here; Speeding Kills)

4. Maintaining active participation in solutions. (participating in a safety camera advocacy campaign)

This multistage approach addresses each audience with compelling messages that advance them to the next stage of engagement. Distributing the messaging of all stages at the same time creates ongoing and progressing levels of engagement. The education campaigns included billboards, bus sides and shelters, radio spots, social media, on-street intercepts and multicultural/ multilingual campaigns. VisionZeroSF.org.

**What Works** Mapping the most dangerous intersections and corridors directed both education and enforcement efforts. • Behavior change campaigns complemented 700 engineering projects, demonstrably decreasing fatailities. • San Francisco's declining fatalities go against national trends; between 2015 and 2016 the National Highway Traffic Safety Administration recorded a 5.6% increase in traffic fatalities.

**Lessons Learned** There were still 20 traffic-related deaths in 2017; people with families and friends whose lives were cut short. There is more work to do. • Billboards and bus shelters were expensive; radio and social media were a more effective media buy.

RIGHT: Project design and photo by MIG, Inc.

FLEXIBLE STREETS

61

LEFT: Insadong-gil, Seoul, South Korea. Photo by Adbar. Licensed under Creative Commons SA 3.0.  RIGHT: High Street, Pottstown, Pennsylvania. Photo by Montgomery County Planning Commission. Licensed under Creative Commons 2.0

New smart technologies are emerging every day. And back-to-basics natural systems of managing water, materials and habitat are becoming more common. Pair them to transform urban infrastructure and create resilient streets everywhere. Each case study provides lessons learned on which to build the best practices included at the end of this chapter. More information can be found at www.reStreets.org.

### INSADONG-GIL PEDESTRIAN STREET  *Seoul, South Korea*

History meets the modern street on this narrow road in a historic district, one of the most popular streets in Seoul. It's home to antique and traditional paper stores, galleries, and tea houses and restaurants, their scents wafting. The asphalt pavement was replaced with flush traditional Korean black granite tiles; paving for autos is rougher compared to the curbless, polished granite pedestrian area. Granite slabs for seating mark a clear path of travel for autos. Street furnishings celebrate historic and modern architecture, with engravings telling the story of the street's past. Gateways and social gathering venues at both ends allow for festivals, calligraphy demonstrations and pansori (music) performances; and the street is closed to traffic on Sunday. The unique streetscape creates both a sensory and historic experience.

### BACK 'ER UP!  *Pottstown, Pennsylvania*

Although it might seem counterintuitive, back-in diagonal parking is proving to be safer than head-in. Similar to parallel parking, cars drive past the stall, stop and back in. They head out with a clear view of oncoming traffic— and bicycles. Pottstown's High Street was an underused 68-foot wide corridor with four lanes of speedy traffic and parallel parking. They wanted to revitalize the Downtown, increase safety, and encourage more pedestrian and bicycle traffic. The solution was to provide 18-feet wide reverse diagonal parking on one side (which increased the amount of parking), parallel parking on the other side, two 6-foot-wide bike lanes, two travel lanes and a center turn lane. That calmed traffic, enhanced walkability and biking, and created a more attractive, intimate corridor that increased retail and economic development.[12]

LEFT: Nørrebrogade, Copenhagen. Photo by Kevin Steinhardt. Licensed under Creative Commons 2.0. CENTER: La Jolla Boulevard and Camino de la Costa, La Jolla, California. Photo by Catherine Courtenaye/MIG, Inc. RIGHT: 15th Street, Washington, DC. Photo by Elvert Barnes. Licensed under Creative Commons 2.0.

### RIDE THE GREEN WAVE  *Nørrebrogade, Copenhagen*

On Nørrebrogade, now said to be the world's busiest bicycle street, biking and walking have priority over cars. The City cut car lane widths in half, while doubling the widths of cycle tracks and sidewalks, and lowering curb heights. Bike at 20 kilometers an hour (radar signals show biking speed) and get "green wave" lights all the way—with green stud lights on the ground to show you're riding the "green wave." There are priority bus lanes with transit stops on medians, no parking along the street, and some sections are car free. Car traffic is down by 60 percent, bicycle use up by 20 percent, pedestrian traffic up by 60 percent. Travel time for buses is down by 10 percent and, amazingly, traffic in the surrounding neighborhood is also down by 10 percent. Plus, there's an increase in commercial activity with streams of people walking and biking.[13]

### LA JOLLA BLVD. ROUNDABOUTS  *San Diego, California*

Pedestrians in San Diego's Bird Rock neighborhood were crossing 68 feet of roadway, often dodging cars traveling 38–42 miles an hour. La Jolla Boulevard, the main vehicle route, was congested, it was hard to park, and caused air pollution. A series of five modern, nicely landscaped roundabouts where the road intersects with collector streets reduces the number of travel lanes from four to two and speeds are controlled at 15–20 mph. Other traffic-calming measures include bulb outs, split hump bumps and 10-feet wide landscaped center medians that serve as pedestrian refuges. A new bike lane is 6–7 feet wide. Diagonal parking on one side and parallel on the other added 30 more parking spaces. The street is now a desirable environment that has activated the area.

### CYCLE TRACKING  *15th Street, Washington, DC*

The first separated bike lanes in the area, 15th Street NW, is a 3.3 mile two-way cycle track between a residential area and Downtown. Tracks are protected by bollards and a parking lane where the traffic is one-way, and by bollards where the street is two-way. The one-way section had been four lanes with a posted speed of 25 and actual observed speeds of 36–45 mph. The District removed one auto lane and, to protect bicyclists at intersections, implemented a bike chicane that shifts cyclists to the line of sight of approaching vehicles, and imposes parking restrictions within 50 feet of the intersection with bike and pedestrian signal phasing. The results: a 40 percent increase in bicycling, slower traffic, and 96 percent of cyclists say it's safer. The track will be extended north.[14]

### WOONERFS, WOOT! *Almere, The Netherlands*

Woonerfs (living streets) developed in Holland, were the inspiration for the Complete Streets movement. After building many separated bike and pedestrian facilities, the Dutch recognized that mode conflicts still existed so they reintegrated everyone back into the roadway. Almere, just outside Amsterdam, was a new development and the entire City design was based on the woonerf concept from the ground up. In residential areas, pedestrians and cyclists have legal priority over motorists. Traffic speeds are reduced significantly, typically below 12 mph. Planters, benches, play equipment, bicycle racks, chicanes and bollards (and sometimes houses) create curves in the travel lanes that break up lines of sight. There are no curbs so everyone is on the same level. And there's spacing between parking to avoid a parking lot feel. Woonerfs have reduced road collisions by 40 percent.[15]

### MORICE TOWN HOME ZONE *Plymouth, England*

Morice Town, within the City of Plymouth, England, was one of nine pilot sites for the 1999 Home Zones program.[16] Home Zone streets have been extensively (and expensively) retrofitted to include shared space, traffic-calming design interventions and landscaping. Community involvement in the design process was also a strong feature. Because home zones often have no clear division between pedestrian space and auto space, vehicles must travel with great caution. There's a 5-mile-per-hour speed limit in the Morice Town shared space (most Home Zones have a 10 mph speed limit). In fact, it's the driver who feels like a "guest" on the road. While Home Zones successfully change the street into shared space, the drawback was high cost—similar improvements are now being done more cost-effectively on other streets.[17]

### TRANSIT GALLERY *Long Beach, California*

You just might miss your bus, ambling along the sandy-textured concrete sidewalk, finding mosaic starfish, crabs and other unexpected sea creatures. This three-block Transit Gallery in downtown Long Beach connects a newly constructed pedestrian promenade, entertainment area, the Convention Center, City Hall, a large bike station, the City-wide bus system and the popular seaside terminus of the Metro line. It reflects a shoreline theme, with eight wave-inspired suspended tensile fabric canopies sheltering free-form seating. The illuminated bus shelter canopies include real-time digital information screens, and new pedestrian lighting between the shelters provides a pleasing nighttime experience. The result is a dramatic, beautiful, identifiable and sustainable transit mall in the heart of the City.

LEFT: Photo by Ann Forsyth.  CENTER: Charlotte Street. Photo by Adrian Trim, Project Manager, Morice Town, Plymouth.  RIGHT: First Street, Long Beach, California. Project design and photo by MIG, Inc.

**TALKING MAPS** *Helsinki, Finland*

BlindSquare, based in Helsinki, uses GPS and Bluetooth Beacons to link with smartphones. It describes the environment, announces points of interest and upcoming street intersections and other user-defined points as one travels or walks by way of a speech synthesizer. People who are blind can plan out a trip before leaving home: find a bus, hail a cab, find and walk to a restaurant or just take a walk. Many functions can be activated by voice commands or touch, using headset controls or the smartphone display. BlindSquare 4.0 now supports indoor Beacon Positioning Systems, for subways, malls and other buildings. Low-energy Bluetooth devices provide both navigation and more detailed messages about shops and museum exhibits. BlindSquare is now in use in 160 countries and 25 languages.

**QR TAG TOUR** *Grand Rapids, Michigan*

Grab a phone and take a history or art walking tour of Downtown Grand Rapids. The City developed tours using QR codes and phones for residents and tourists to find information about specific stops and art installments on the route, audio histories of the location or art, links to find other places nearby, and a walking map to the next stop. Users can even ask for directions to the first stop to be texted to them before leaving home or their hotel. They're also encouraged to submit their own photos along the route for others to see on social media. Signs at key locations also provide a url for those who don't have QR readers.

**SENSORY IMMERSION** *Madurai, India*

The sacred City of Madurai on the southern Indian peninsula is a major site for Hindu celebration. The City is organized around a central temple complex. Approximately 25,000 people per day move along the roads—guided by smells, sounds and sights—on their way to the religious sites. The names of the streets become unimportant. The closer one gets to a religious site, the greater is the presence and availability of incense, oils, coconuts, camphor, flowers for offerings and other scented religious elements from street vendors. Street hawkers emerge, along with waves of bright colors, drummers and chiming temple bells. Paving materials and patterns change from asphalt and concrete to cobblestones, discernible to people wearing shoes or barefoot. Finally, one comes upon the ornate gopuram towers, visual markers that orient travelers in any part of the City.

The design and location of physical elements can encourage new activities and change behavior. Marked bike lanes and bike prioritization signals induce people to bike because they feel safe and comfortable. Combining elements such as medians, trees, lighting and sidewalk extensions slows down traffic on flexible streets. And, on some streets, signage might not be needed at all.

## Auditory wayfinding

Talking signs deliver voice messages to handheld devices via infrared pulses. Audio maps and signs, singing water features, piped music, and talking signals can locate landmarks, buildings and hazards.

## Bike amenities

Bike racks, enclosed storage, and rental and repair facilities encourage more bicyclists to use the street. Marked bike lanes separate bikes from vehicular and pedestrian pathways.

## Landmarks

Gateways, memorials, fountains, street arches, statues and planting designs mark a significant intersection or street area and can help those with cognitive disabilities mark a path.

## Lane closure devices

To calm and direct traffic, choose roundabouts, speed bumps or chicanes depending on traffic speed and the size of the intersection or roadway.

## Lighting

Important for nighttime visibility and a sense of security, custom lighting can help create a distinctive identity.

## Medians

Planted or paved medians can be located in the middle of the road or at the side of the road, separating a bike lane or pedestrian path, as part of multi-way boulevards.

## Planter boxes

Movable planter boxes with wheels can be placed strategically to redirect traffic for temporary lane closures.

## Sidewalk extensions

Bulb outs at intersections or mid-block reduce crosswalk distances, calm traffic and provide space for other types of street functions. They can be constructed or simply striped.

## Signage

Signs should be made of durable, non-reflective materials with high-contrast printing including stop signs, street names, directional, regulatory/safety and informational (maps, interpretive orientation, schedules, routes) signs.

## Signaling devices

Traffic signals are usually positioned at road intersections, pedestrian crossings and other locations to control competing flows of traffic. Bike prioritization signals and crossing can help bicyclists feel safe.

## Bollards

Retractable or removable bollards can temporarily close lanes or entire streets for events.

## Crosswalks

Marked crosswalks direct the path of pedestrian travel at intersections and, in long blocks, between intersections so drivers are aware that pedestrians can cross.

## Flexible lanes

Bike, parking, vehicular traffic and public transit lanes can be dedicated to one mode permanently or temporarily through lane indicators, such as striping and smart studs.

## Furniture

Movable custom furniture provides maximum flexibility and adds to the area's identity. Trash receptacles help maintain a clean and attractive space.

## Olfactory Wayfinding

Smell is the strongest sense; scented trees, flowers and herbs; outdoor fruit and vegetable displays; and outdoor dining can help people navigate and understand their environment.

## Parking lanes

Permanent or temporary parking can be parallel, angled head-in or angled rear-in, providing loading and unloading areas, and can be temporarily blocked off for other uses during non-peak times.

## Paving

A variety of paving types can differentiate pedestrian areas from roadways or bike lanes, provide safety surfacing and visual interest—all at street level.

## Pedestrian paths of travel

Sidewalks, escalators, marked paths, etc. direct pedestrian traffic to suitable crossing points and separate them from vehicular and bike travel.

## Tactile safety

Elements such as ground plane materials, truncated domes, etc., create a shoreline for people with visual impairments.

## Tactile wayfinding

Motion/pressure detectors, tactile 3D maps and braille signage can help people with visual impairments navigate.

## Transit stops

Public transit routes served by buses, streetcars and light rail designate a place for passenger loading or unloading.

## Trees and vegetation

Trees, shrubs and grasses can be located in planting strips and in medians to calm traffic, provide an island for pedestrians and increase green space.

FLEXIBLE STREETS

67

# CREATING A FLEXIBLE STREET

It's important to ensure that streets respect the desired role and character of the neighborhood, including the type and intensity of land use, urban form, the desired activities on the sidewalk (see the following chapters for many types of activities on sidewalks and streets) and the overall safety and comfort of all travel modes. By designing flexible streets, communities can accommodate increasing multimodal mobility needs and technological advances, and allow for more placemaking and wayfinding opportunities.

The overarching best practice is to design level streets without curbs, using flexible barriers such as retractable bollards and planter boxes to demarcate a curb zone. That allows the pedestrian areas, bike lanes, parking lanes and travel lanes to change at specific times or according to traffic needs. Low-cost solutions like restriping for narrower lane widths or to create bicycle lanes can also be applied.

While not every street is appropriate as a flexible street, the following best practices can help increase multimodal connectivity.

LEFT: Marich Way and Karen Way, Mountain View, California. Photo by Catherine Courtenaye/MIG, Inc.    RIGHT: Pearl Street District, Portland, Oregon. Photo by Google Maps 2017.

# Improve street network connectivity

① Align and connect all new streets in public and private projects with existing public streets.

② Where possible, enhance connectivity in existing residential neighborhoods by providing pedestrian and bicycle connector paths between cul-de-sacs and adjoining community destinations or nearby roads. These connector paths could be created by repurposing existing easements or as part of voluntary or mandatory retrofits when adjoining properties are redeveloped.

③ Where possible, enhance multimodal connectivity in residential and non-residential streets by incorporating multiuse paths. These paths should provide access for pedestrians and bicyclists, and for emergency providers and low-volume destination traffic; they can be stand-alone or part of park-like open spaces such as greenways. All improvements should enhance the overall park-friendly character by incorporating trees, planting, pavers, etc.

④ Establish a street connectivity ordinance customized to local conditions (topography, natural features, climate, historical precedence), to create optimum length of blocks and increase the number of intersections (maximum 1/4 mile between full movement intersections). Length of blocks could range from approximately 200 feet to 600 feet or 1,600 linear feet perimeter.

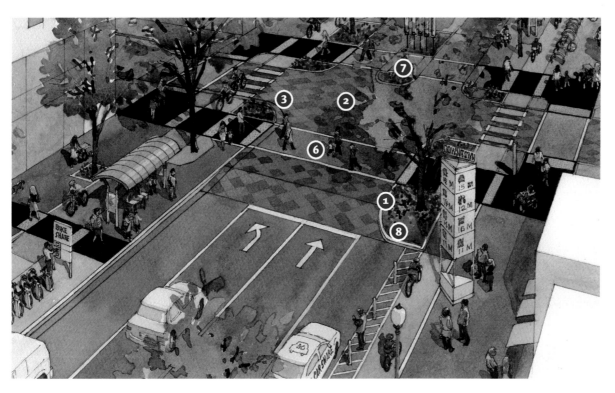

## Emphasize safety for all users

**1** Make intersections as compact as possible and avoid free-flowing movements.

**2** Design intersections at or close to right angles. Use elements such as bulb outs to redesign skewed intersections. Negotiate with adjoining property owners to obtain easements if necessary.

**3** Design corner radii to minimize crossing distances and slow vehicular turning speeds.

**4** Allow larger, infrequent service/emergency vehicles to encroach upon multiple departure lanes and part way into opposing travel lanes.

**5** Allow pedestrian crossings on all legs of an intersection, unless there are no pedestrian access destinations on or near one or more of the corners.

**6** Place crosswalks as close as possible to the desired line of pedestrians, generally aligned with the opposing sidewalk.

**7** Create pedestrian refuges if the crossing distance exceeds 40 feet.

**8** Provide curb extensions to replace the parking lane at crosswalks to reduce pedestrian crossing distances and improve visibility between pedestrians and vehicles.

## Design to calm traffic

LEFT: College Street and South 11th Avenue, Bozeman, Montana. Photo by MIG, Inc.   RIGHT: West Capitol Avenue, Sacramento. Project design and photo by MIG, Inc.

**1** Provide 9- to 10-foot wide travel lanes for street speeds of 25 mph or less. Provide 10- to 11-foot wide travel lanes for speeds of 30–35 mph.

**2** Use on-street parking to help achieve desired travel speeds.

**3** Include the width of the gutter pan when measuring lane widths for vehicles, bicyclists and parking.

**4** Provide trees in medians and along sidewalks to provide a sense of enclosure.

**5** Consider the use of bulb outs, chicanes, mini roundabouts and traffic circles to calm traffic.

**6** Correct deficiencies and provide streetscape enhancements such as temporary bulb outs and enhanced crosswalks when repaving or restriping streets.

## Prioritize walking as a primary mode

**1** Ensure universal access for people of all abilities.

**2** Provide a minimum 5-foot wide sidewalk on streets with a relatively low volume of foot traffic and a minimum 8-foot wide sidewalk on streets with relatively high volume.

**3** Ensure that sidewalk cross slopes are no greater than 2 percent.

**4** Enhance the pedestrian environment by providing amenities and protection from the elements, such as trees, shelters, street lighting, etc.

**5** Ensure that uncontrolled crossing distances are no more than 21 feet.

**6** Eliminate or minimize the use of double or triple left (or right) turn lanes at signalized intersections.

**7** Time signals to minimize pedestrian wait time (ideally no more than 90 seconds).

**8** Provide and set back 12- to 24-inch wide advance yield/stop lines at signalized intersections 4 feet to 10 feet from the crosswalk.

FLEXIBLE STREETS

73

## Prioritize biking as a primary mode

**1** Create a system of designated bicycle facilities that give priority to bicyclists. Add curvilinear elements to prevent cars from using protected bike facilities.

**2** Use pavement markings, such as sharrows and colored pavement, to signify bike lanes.

**3** Discourage through-motor-vehicle traffic on designated bicycle boulevards.

**4** Locate bike lanes on higher volume (more than 3000–5000 vehicles per day) or high-speed (greater than 30 mph) roads.

**5** If on-street parking is permitted, provide a minimum 6-foot bike lane between travel and parking lanes. Increase width to 8 feet to mitigate higher speeds and volumes.

**6** Provide a 4- to 6-foot wide shoulder to accommodate bicycles on rural roads.

**7** Provide about 8-foot wide cycle tracks or protected bike lanes in urban areas to minimize pedestrian conflicts. Minimize pedestrian crossings, driveways and loading and unloading activity.

**8** Provide sufficient space for street cleaning equipment.

**9** Create buffered bike lanes on wide, busy streets, where physical separation of bike lanes and cycle tracks is not feasible due to frequent pedestrian crossings, driveways, loading zones cost, or operational and maintenance requirements. Slow traffic by narrowing the adjoining travel lanes, and provide a painted divider between bike lanes and travel lanes.

10 On constrained right-of-way streets without on-street parking where bike lanes are not possible, provide 14-feet to 15-feet wide curb lanes. Use striping to separate cyclists and pedestrians, to discourage motorists from driving there and to reduce traffic speeds.

11 For streets with constrained rights-of-way, where bike lanes are not possible, provide an 11- to 12-foot wide right lane with a shared-lane marking for the cyclist outside the car door zone.

12 Provide 12-foot wide shared-use paths in areas where pedestrians and bicyclists need to share the path of travel.

13 Design intersections to reduce conflicts among travel modes by heightening visibility, denoting a clear right-of-way, and ensuring that all users are aware of each other.

14 Continue marked bicycle facilities at intersections (up to crosswalk) and, where needed, place a bike lane pocket between the right turn lane and the rightmost through lane.

15 Incorporate bicycle detection and bicycle signal heads at signalized intersections.

16 Locate bicycle parking at major destinations.

17 Provide bike-sharing programs.

# Develop on-street parking strategies

**1** Create parking with flexible multi-purpose lanes that in the future can serve other uses, such as outdoor dining or stormwater management.

**2** Locate on-street parking to help reduce travel speeds by narrowing the travel lanes.

**3** Explore angled parking where there is a need to maximize on-street parking.

**4** Provide back-in diagonal parking on roads with on-street bike lanes to improve driver visibility.

**5** Utilize advance parking systems to guide drivers in congested areas to the nearest parking space or facility with empty parking spaces via cellphone, smartphone or GPS navigation device. This reduces congestion and illegally parked cars, as well as wasted time and fuel.

**6** Encourage payment for parking via smartphone for initial payment and additional time so drivers pay only for time actually parked and receive text message reminders, reducing citations.

**7** Create a variable rate parking policy; price parking to create some available spaces most of the time, increasing parking availability and turnover.

**8** Survey average space occupancy at least annually and adjust the metered parking rates up or down in $0.25 intervals to achieve the target occupancy rate.

**9** Provide appropriate ADA parking spaces *on every block*.

**10** Actively involve the adjoining merchants and property owners in the development and maintenance of any new parking occupancy policy.

## Provide wayfinding cues

**1** Limit the number of wayfinding features and the amount of content; too many elements can be confusing and ambiguous.

**2** Select materials and surfaces to create durable, low-glare, high-contrast and vandal-proof wayfinding elements.

**3** Ensure that the placement height, distance, orientation, approach and print size of wayfinding materials make them accessible for all users.

**4** Create logos or icons that reference widely recognized features of the surrounding area.

**5** Choose colors and typefaces that reflect the area's physical and cultural context, ensuring they are compatible with print and mobile media.

**6** Use heads-up mapping in which north, south, east or west are rotated to correspond with the direction the user is facing.

**7** Use a minimalist approach for urban corridors with significant views; let the destination speak for itself.

**8** Use internationally recognizable symbols and provide appropriate translation.

**9** Provide test periods for temporary signage elements before permanent systems are installed.

**10** Develop municipal codes that encourage private realm signage to complement rather than compete with public wayfinding.

**11** Provide a way to collect real-time user feedback on wayfinding and interpretive features using mobile technology apps.

**12** Establish procedures and allocate funding for maintenance and updating of wayfinding content and features.

**13** Use dynamic wayfinding technology when location information changes frequently.

## Use multiple, multisensory wayfinding cues

(1) Use combinations of explicit and implicit wayfinding features to direct foot traffic, for example, pairing print signage with linear planting, lighting or paving.

(2) Provide a clear, unambiguous "shoreline" to provide cues to visually impaired people, with accessible textured paving materials such as decomposed granite, treated wood or stone pavers that contrast with common ADA-compliant surfaces.

(3) Integrate location or QR codes or an app to provide translations, more information or to gamify and activate a place with retail coupons, virtual scavenger hunts and interactive contests.

(4) Use emerging talking-sign technology for both mobile devices and at destinations.

(5) Develop a signage system with primary information in tactile, olfactory or audio form, supplemented with written and visual elements.

(6) For food-focused destination streets, develop interpretive signage that capitalizes on pleasing, attractive smells.

(7) Use different types of scented landscape elements to distinguish different streets. Fragrant trees, herbs and flowers can denote key nodes and distinctive streets.

(8) In hot, dry climates, incorporate misters and other water spray elements.

LEFT: Water Street, Vancouver, British Columbia. Photo by MIG, Inc.   RIGHT: Wind chimes, North Liberty Street, Downtown Arts District, Winston-Salem, North Carolina. Photo by MIG, Inc.

(9) Along historic streets, integrate historic video footage or tactile features such as period-specific paving or seating to tell the story of past eras.

(10) In historic districts, find a predominant smell, sound or sensation that can be linked to interpretive signage features.

(11) Combine fountains and other water features with an audio element to enhance the perception of landmarks.

(12) Combine iconic elements such as clock towers with visual features like steam or audio to celebrate the history of a neighborhood or to denote primary gathering areas.

(13) In windy climates, combine sculptural elements such as wind chimes and other wind-activated instruments into street furniture, such as streetlights, to create soothing sounds and to celebrate key destinations.

(14) In dense urban environments, design certain nodes or streets to be sunny and warm and others to be cool and shaded.

FLEXIBLE STREETS

79

# Design local shared streets

LEFT, RIGHT: Nueva Street, San Antonio. Project design and photos by MIG, Inc.

**1** Locate shared streets, which allow both pedestrians and vehicles to move freely within the entire street right-of-way, where there is low traffic, a historical precedence, traditional community patterns and a need or willingness to share the road.

**2** Design streets to accommodate the right mix of traffic volumes (not more than 3000 to 5000 vehicles per day) and traffic speeds (15 mph or less) to mitigate impacts to the free flow of pedestrians.

**3** Design streets with level surfaces so that the street surface is not physically divided into areas of use by curbs or level differences.

**4** Integrate "Naked Street" principles (minimal use of traffic signs, road markings and other traffic management features) to help drivers recognize that the street is not a typical road, and that they should drive more slowly.

**5** On level streets, address needs of visually impaired people, children and people with restricted mobility to ensure that they are not put at increased risk. Provide a contiguous 5-foot wide ADA-accessible path with appropriate cues such as bollards, truncated domes, etc., at intersections.

**6** Reduce traffic management features that tend to encourage users of vehicles.

## Design multi-way boulevards

**1** Design a central roadway with 10–11-foot wide through lanes operating at 30–45 mph. More specifics can be found in *The Boulevard Book* by Allan B. Jacobs, Elizabeth MacDonald and Yodan Rofé.

**2** Design the side access roads for neighborhood commercial and residential use operating at 10–20 mph, with a 7-foot wide street parking lane and a 9–10-foot wide shared vehicle and bike travel lane.

**3** Prioritize space for medians over sidewalks—especially side medians—to allow space for canopy trees, street lighting, bus stops with seating and shelters and pedestrian refuge areas. Ideally, medians should be 10 to 30 feet wide to allow for trees, strolling, gathering areas and signage.

**4** Enhance the pedestrian-friendly character of side access roads through special paving.

## Design for autonomous cars

**1** Design roads for both partial and complete integration of autonomous cars. Ensure that autonomous cars improve the safety of all users—especially pedestrians and bicyclists— by reducing speeds, narrowing travel lanes and reducing turning radii.

**2** Re-purpose the roadway space gained from narrowing lanes and reducing turning radii to provide extra space for non-motorized uses such as bike lanes, wider sidewalks, planting, urban greening, social gathering, etc.

**3** Compliment new car technology with new traffic signal technology to reduce or eliminate collisions caused by human error.

**4** Ensure that autonomous cars improve multimodal access opportunities for the most vulnerable users, who have traditionally not been equal users of the street (e.g., seniors and those with visual or hearing impairments).

**5** Develop policies and infrastructure that encourage using shared cars and bikes to access transit (closing "the last mile"), enhancing travel times for everyone.

LEFT: Nueva Street, San Antonio. Project design and photo by MIG, Inc.

## Integrate technology into street design

( 1 ) When feasible, synchronize signals to support efficient movement of cars.

( 2 ) Provide short signal cycle lengths, which allow frequent opportunities to cross major roadways.

( 3 ) Ensure that signal timing does not hinder bicycle and foot traffic or provide insufficient crossing times.

( 4 ) Display the pedestrian WALK sign 2 to 5 seconds prior to the green for vehicles so pedestrians enter the crosswalk before drivers begin to turn, increasing their chances of being seen by drivers.

( 5 ) Prohibit right turn on red if there are restricted sight lines between motorists and pedestrians.

( 6 ) Use pedestrian user-friendly intelligent (PUFFIN) signals, which detect slower pedestrians in crosswalks and add clearance interval time to the pedestrian signals.

( 7 ) Use pedestrian scrambles (diagonal crossings with all vehicles stopped) if turning vehicles conflict with very high pedestrian volumes.

( 8 ) In urban areas and at locations with many crossing pedestrians, time the pedestrian phase to be on automatic recall, so pedestrians do not have to push a button to activate the signals.

( 9 ) Use reversible lanes to increase directional roadway capacity.

( 10 ) Consider inductive power on-road lights that allow lanes to be opened and closed based on varying traffic patterns.

( 11 ) Identify areas for charging electric vehicles.

( 12 ) Provide on-road, dynamic route information panels and variable speed control signs to communicate information on congestion and incidents.

## Provide information to travelers *before* they embark

**1** Monitor individual streets and the larger street network based on real-time conditions to develop solutions for integrating real-time traffic management and travel demand management (TDM).

**2** Enhance traditional TDM such as rideshare matching, promotion of alternative modes and vanpool provisions.

**3** Use flexible high occupancy/toll and express lanes, and expanded park and ride systems to modulate automobile use on major corridors.

**4** Provide real-time pre-trip traveler information systems to encourage more efficient travel, suggesting routes and times of the day that are less congested.

**5** Provide pre-trip and on-trip information to influence mode choice. Provide travel time for drivers stuck in traffic if they were to shift to a nearby park-and-ride service.

**6** Enhance real-time traffic management strategies, such as alternative routes and improved public transportation facilities, to mitigate traffic during major construction projects and during large events.

**7** Explore road-pricing schemes (congestion pricing) to reduce private automobile access in congested urban centers, with incentives for changing modes or time of travel. Revenue can be used to improve transit services and provide free or discounted transit passes.

**8** Provide incentives for bike-sharing and car-sharing programs.

## Engage the community

**1** Involve the community early on in planning and design of streets and streetscapes through community meetings, design charrettes, websites, online surveys, blogs, pop-up demonstrations, etc.

**2** Build partnerships with residents and businesses so that they can learn about the benefits of streetscape improvements.

**3** Require local businesses to contribute to the cost of certain streetscape improvements, such as trees, shrubs, seating, etc.

**4** For relatively new concepts such as back-in parking and roundabouts, create a temporary situation on the site so people can experience the new concept before it is finalized.

**5** For long-term maintenance, create a volunteer program with community members, local organizations and community groups. Identify a volunteer coordinator to interact with the agency responsible for streetscape improvements.

## ADELINE STREET

*South Side, Berkeley, California*

This street incorporates flexible, multiple modes:

- It's a major pedestrian and bike corridor with fast moving traffic; its wide streets allow for protected bike facilities while providing tree-lined, comfortable sidewalks.
- Its large central median can be transformed into a park and used for gathering and temporary community events.

Pop-up events were used to test ideas and determine which ones met with community acceptance.

# 4

# GATHER ON THE STREET

*Social Streets*

At a party, a good host greets people, makes them feel welcome, makes connections between people and animates the group. The host prepares the space, creates a welcoming environment and sets the stage for social interaction. A good street can do the same.

Once upon a time, street life was an integral part of neighborhood social life. Friends hung out, children played, neighbors stayed in touch, strangers met and people watched people. Streets were equalizers; everybody was on the street. Then came the surge of motorized vehicles, and everything changed.

In the United States, the case was made that the main function of a street was to move vehicles. Social activities on the street would block traffic, impede business, attract people who might commit crimes and increase city liability and maintenance costs. Gradually, we stopped using our streets to socialize, perhaps allowing a street closure once a year for a 4th of July parade.

As we lost communal streets, we lost invaluable connections with our environment and with each other. Donald Appleyard's seminal study *Livable Streets* showed that social connections between people on a street are inversely proportionate to the amount of traffic.[1]

**WHY GATHER ON THE STREET?**

Social streets can play the important role of the "third place"—a place between home and workplace (or home and school)—encouraging broader, more creative interactions in a free, non-privatized environment. A well-designed social street becomes a great outdoor living room, welcoming people of all genders, races, ethnicity, ages and socio-economic levels.

While people today may seem to be buried in personal technology and disconnected from each other, actually the opposite is true. People could use their laptops and tablets at home, but instead they are using them in parks and at cafes. They have woven technology into their environment because they do feel a need to be with people. And that technology can be used to bring them closer together on the street.

Social gathering on our streets can also help break through one of the major issues in our cities: how to improve a community physically and economically without alienating those who already live there. As new residents move in, there is often little connection between them and their neighbors, which results in friction and misunderstandings. Streets can become places to participate in the life of the community.

Social hub streets create opportunities to meet the neighbors; they convey a sense of belonging and build trust amongst the community's inhabitants. The social space can reflect and coalesce the identity of the community's historical occupants, new residents, businesses and visitors. That creates "social capital," which can be called on when the community needs to work together to address issues and solve problems.

Being connected to the community in small and big ways also has a positive influence on mental well-being. And, having more people on the street at various times of the day and night increases both actual safety and the perception of safety in the area.

The social gathering function of a street underpins all the other street functions explored in the following chapters. It's worth examining specifically how to design and develop the right framework for social spaces that balances the needs of vehicular traffic, pedestrian safety and comfort, and a connection to adjoining land uses. Streets designed for social gathering will put people

SOCIAL STREETS

before cars and overcome the barriers to bringing life back to the street.

## GREAT STREET SPACES

Social gathering can happen in existing plazas and malls, but there are also underutilized spaces such as bulb outs and medians, and even temporary or permanent encroachments into travel lanes. The street can offer a diversity of safe and desirable spaces that facilitate and accommodate a wide range of human interaction. And it can allow for uses that change with time of day, day of the week and the season. Three types of locations are most conducive:

- **Street corridors:** Whether a few blocks of one street or a series of interconnected streets, different sections and corridors of streets can serve many events such as street fairs, Ciclovías and parades. A primary street with branches of intersecting cross streets can provide additional event space, as well as extend connectivity to neighborhoods. Loop routes provide good physical environments for parades, races, marches, and exercise programs that are based on walking and biking.

- **Sidewalks and parking lanes:** Wide sidewalks are suitable for many small events, such as exercise programs and small markets. In combination with temporarily closed parking lanes, they can expand to accommodate larger events such as farmers markets, performances and food stalls.

- **Nodes:** Plazas, pocket parks, bulb outs and other spaces can host a linked series of small-scale events such as exercise programs, street performances and meet-ups. They can also be a place for permanent small-scale ongoing events that can coexist with other day-to-day street functions.

## GOALS

Social gathering streets should aim to meet the following overall goals:

- Engage people and encourage them to return.

- Celebrate community, neighborhoods, cultural values and diversity, people and accomplishments.

- Create social interactions and build social capital by enhancing connections between individuals and the larger community and promoting community pride and ownership.

FACING: Bell Street, Seattle, Washington. Project design and photo by MIG, Inc.

GATHER · SHOP · PLAY · GROW · GREEN · MOVE ·

**GATHER**
Learning · Parading · Eating · Talking · Sitting · Meeting · Playing music · Singing · Demonstrating · Dancing · People watching · Networking · Teaching · Resting

**SHOP**
Manufacturing · Dining · Producing · Cooking · Browsing · Buying · Displaying · Bartering · Performing · Bargaining · Selling

**PLAY**
Sliding · Thinking · Jumping · Geocaching · Drawing · Exercising · Reading · Building · Discovering · Balancing · Playing games · Climbing · Sensing

**GROW**
Storing · Harvesting · Composting · Pruning · Propagating · Weeding · Planting · Mulching · Irrigating

**GREEN**
Rejuvenating · Harvesting water · Managing waste · Reusing · Recycling · Creating habitat · Generating energy · Distributing materials · Cleansing water

**MOVE**
Locating · Rolling/skating · Navigating · Strolling · Servicing · Walking · Driving · Riding · Biking · Orienting · Running · Interpreting · Parking

### ACTIVITIES ON THE SOCIAL STREET

Social streets draw people in and help them gather and interact formally in planned activities, and spontaneously. Choose and combine social activities as appropriate for different types of streets, keeping in mind that the same streets can also include activities such as play and commerce.

# TYPES OF SOCIAL GATHERING EVENTS

Streets can be designed for both programmed social gathering—a street fair, parade or special event—and spontaneous social gathering.

Currently, most spontaneous interactions on streets are pure serendipity, a chance meeting with a friend or coworker, a few words spoken, and the encounter is over. But create a concentration of accessible space, physical elements, programming and technology, and the result is a social space that encourages people to stop and linger—even to return on other occasions and perhaps bring their families. The street becomes a stage set, providing cues that lead people to interact with the street and each other. When a city or town provides the infrastructure to make the area "sticky" and the events or programming to draw people, the community will use the space to gather.

Allan Jacobs said it well in his book *Great Streets:* "First and foremost, a great street should help make a community and facilitate people acting and interacting to achieve in concert what they might not achieve alone....The best streets will be those where it is possible to see other people and to meet all kinds of people, not just of one class or color or age. The best streets encourage participation."[2]

The wide variety of social gatherings, their diversity in scale and their temporal nature allow streets to be constantly reconsidered and repurposed to meet changing needs. Following are some of the common types of organized events.

TOP ROW, LEFT TO RIGHT: Photo by MIG, Inc. • Women's March on Washington. "IMG_0849, Saturday, January 21, 2017, Washington, DC." Photo by Aimee Custis. Licensed under Creative Commons 2.0 • Photo by Bradley P. Johnson/Open Streets Mpls / Minneapolis Bicycle Coalition 163/365. "These folks took open streets to a whole new level." Licensed under Creative Commons 2.0 • Photo by Dan Flies. "Block Party, IMG_6475.JPG." Licensed under Creative Commons 2.0 • Ciclovía. Photo by Open Streets Mpls / Minneapolis Bicycle Coalition • "08a.PopUpSkateArtMusic.Funk. WDC.2May2015." Photo by Elvert Barnes. Licensed under Creative Commons 2.0.
BOTTOM ROW, LEFT TO RIGHT: Photo by izu navi. Licensed under Creative Commons 2.0 • London tour. Photo by Marcin Wichary. Licensed under Creative Commons 2.0 • Missoula, Montana, Farmers Market. Photo by Catherine Courtenaye. • Street Play. Photo by Open Streets Mpls / Minneapolis Bicycle Coalition • Artmurmur, Oakland, California. Photo by Sonny Abesamis. Licensed under Creative Commons 2.0 • Marathon, Taiwan. Photo by MiNe. Licensed under Creative Commons 2.0.

## Busking

Buskers—musicians, magicians, mimes and other street entertainers—perform alone or in a group and usually receive tips from their audiences. Some municipalities provide designated spaces and require permits; others allow more spontaneous performances.

## Demonstrations/Marches

Sometimes organized with official permits or convened as an act of civil disobedience to express a sentiment about an issue or cause.

## Fairs and Parades

These events are usually focused on a theme, holiday, neighborhood, or cultural group and can be large, multiday, ticketed events on closed streets or a couple of hours on a single block. They often include vendors with a range of food, products and services.

## Interpretive Tours

Programs can be organized or self-initiated, based on a theme, history, trees, art, paranormal activities, etc. They can be led by a docent/tour guide or conducted simply using maps and cell phones.

### Exercise Events

Sometimes sponsored by government agencies or nonprofit organizations, linear events can promote walking or biking at specific times for specific groups or teams, often with prizes and recognition.

### Neighborhood Block Parties

Block parties are often small-scale events on a single closed block where neighbors join to BBQ, play games, have fun and build community. Neighborhood organizations usually plan and host, following guidelines set forth by local municipalities.

### Open Streets

Sometimes called Ciclovías (or Raahgiri in India), they involve temporarily closing entire streets or specific traffic lanes to motorized vehicles and are usually held on a fixed day of the week or on designated days during specified hours.

### Pop-Up Events

Temporary events such as art displays, flash mobs, concerts, food stands and mini-festivals can pop up on underutilized sidewalks, bulb outs and alleys.

### Public Markets

Farmers and other vendors can sell goods directly to the public, usually at a specified location where the street is closed. They are regulated by municipalities and usually managed by a nonprofit agency. They often become small festivals with live entertainment.

### Street Play

Organized by municipalities or nonprofit groups to prioritize playing on the street during certain hours or certain days. Formal play street programs usually occur on closed streets, but shared streets— when combined with public awareness efforts—can also be successful (see also "Play on the Street").

### Progressive Events

An organized series of activities and destinations centered on a program theme such as an art walk, garden tours and food events, participants bike or walk between venues. Entertainment and refreshments are often offered at booths or by restaurants along the route.

### Races/Walks

Ranging from marathons to family strolls, races and walks usually take place on streets that are fully or partially closed to auto traffic. They often promote a festive atmosphere along the route as crowds gather; there may be live entertainment and vendors along the route or at the finish line.

## SUNNYSIDE PIAZZA

*Portland, Oregon*

Sometimes all it takes is a coat of paint. Sunnyside Piazza is an inner Portland street intersection that surrounding neighbors converted into a community gathering space.

Sunnyside is a moderate-income urban neighborhood with about 3,500 households. Neighbors complained about noise, speeding, drugs and abandoned cars. In 2001, they got energized by City Repair, a local nonprofit that helps residents design and build social gathering spaces in their neighborhoods.[3] City Repair began as a grassroots movement when, in response to an unauthorized gathering, the City said: "That land is public space. Nobody can use it." Portland now allows community groups to create public realm projects, following City guidelines.

Residents painted a giant sunflower in the middle of the intersection, turning it into a piazza that increases attention on the street. One neighbor provided 28 gallons of paint. Others placed planter barrels at the four corners to keep people from parking in the piazza and to slow traffic down.

The next year, the City approved trellises on the corners, now planted with honeysuckle. Residents created an art wall made of cob—a traditional building material of clay, sand, straw and water—with colorful mosaics and

SOCIAL STREETS

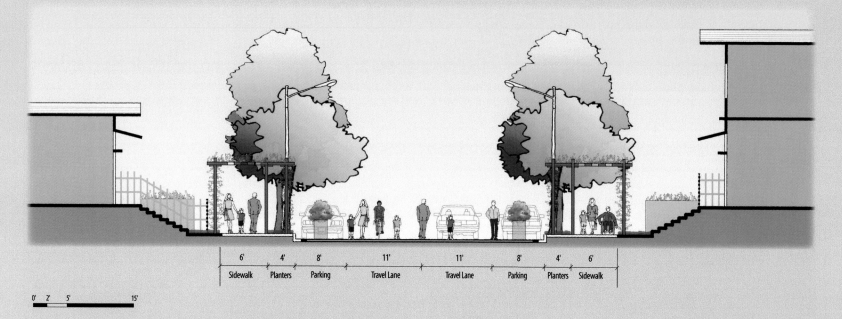

6' Sidewalk | 4' Planters | 8' Parking | 11' Travel Lane | 11' Travel Lane | 8' Parking | 4' Planters | 6' Sidewalk

0'  2'  5'          15'

SOCIAL STREETS

*100*

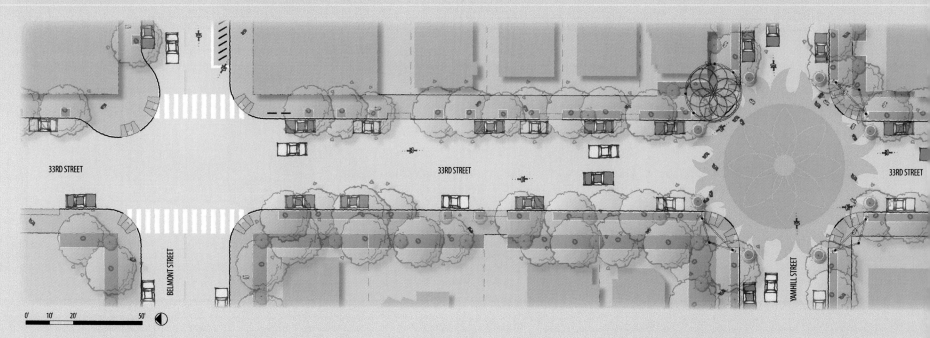

33RD STREET

33RD STREET

33RD STREET

BELMONT STREET

YAMHILL STREET

0'  10'  20'        50'

niches for sitting. A cob information kiosk holds messages and notices. And a solar-powered fountain and wishing pond invites passersby to pause. Neighbors raised the money and did all the work.

A study by Portland State University in April 2003 showed 32 percent of pedestrians stopped and interacted with the piazza.[4] Joggers took an extra few laps around the flower, and both walking and biking traffic was higher than before the painting. The survey showed that 65 percent of Sunnyside Piazza-area residents rated their neighborhood an excellent place to live, compared with 35 percent at another similar but unimproved intersection. Calls for police services have decreased noticeably since the intersection repair.

Sunnyside Piazza remains a catalyst for sidewalk conversations, with major community events two to three times a year.

**What Works** All the improvements were very low cost. • The act of creating the piazza itself expanded social networks and increased social capital. • With more attention and activity on the street, crime rates have decreased. • The intersection is still completely usable by cars but their speeds have been reduced.

**Lessons Learned** There have been a few acts of vandalism, although not very serious. • There is a problem with litter, but neighbors pitch in to clean up. • The paint needs to be refreshed to keep it looking attractive.

## PUBLIC PARKLETS

*San Francisco, California*

Parklets are aesthetic enhancements to the streetscape that encourage people to linger. They usually repurpose two or three parking spots along a block, building out a platform so that the grade of the sidewalk gets carried out into the parking lane, such as on 18th St. in San Francisco. Benches, planters, landscaping, bike parking, artwork, tables and seating come together to provide a welcoming new public space. They're well-demarcated areas where families can feel separated from cars and socialize—and by extension also support nearby retail.

San Francisco was determined to transform its "sea of asphalt," through parklets projects—low-cost and built by "sponsors" without any public funding.[5] Sponsors are usually a business or a business district, although access cannot be limited to customers—parklets remain part of the public realm, open to all passersby.

The City Planning Department worked with communities to construct the first five parklets in 2010, then began accepting proposals for sponsor-led parklet installations. The City developed design guidelines and a complete manual to guide the process.[6]

Sponsors are responsible for designing and constructing their own parklet space. A wide

SOCIAL STREETS

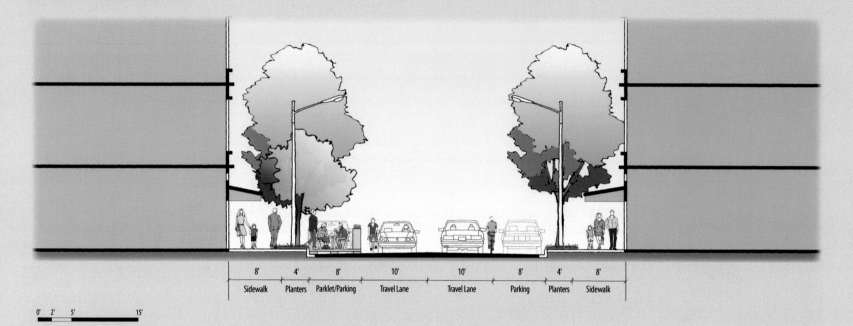

| 8' | 4' | 8' | 10' | 10' | 8' | 4' | 8' |
|----|----|----|-----|-----|----|----|----|
| Sidewalk | Planters | Parklet/Parking | Travel Lane | Travel Lane | Parking | Planters | Sidewalk |

0'  2'  5'          15'

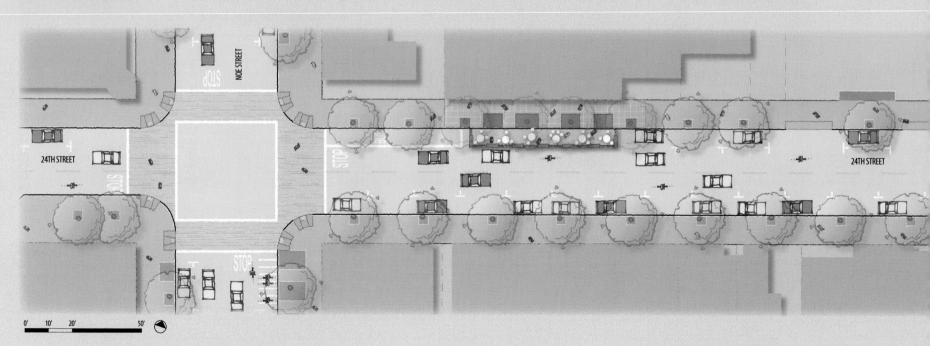

0'  10'  20'          50'

range of design is allowed so each parklet can reflect the creativity and diversity of the area. Sponsors must include letters of community support in their permit application. They also assume liability for the parklet and must keep it in good repair. The City monitors parklets and conducts annual reviews to ensure they're well maintained and accessible. The City charges nominal fees for an application and site inspection, a fee for removing two parking meters and a small annual fee. The City has found parklets work best in the middle of streets with low speed limits.

A study in Philadelphia by University City District, a nonprofit neighborhood development organization, found that parklets attract an even mix of men and women, indicating that they are safe and welcoming spaces.[7] And 20 to 30 percent of users were not customers of adjacent businesses, answering concerns that the creation of a parklet removes street space from the public realm for the sole benefit of a private business. San Francisco gives priority to applications from nonprofits, community groups and cultural institutions.[8]

RIGHT: Ourcadia Parklet, Post Street, San Francisco. Project design by Ogrydziak Prillinger Architects (www.oparch.net). Photo © Tim Griffith

**What Works** Community members get to know each other and have an enhanced sense of pride in the area. • Increased space for people in the public realm encourages lingering and socializing. • Merchants are increasingly convinced that taking away a few parking spaces results in higher foot traffic. • Public-private partnerships often result in improved community relations.

**Lessons Learned** Some incidents of poor maintenance and lack of funding have been reported. • Businesses report that parklets do not necessarily attract more customers, but do strengthen community connections. • Because they are usually funded by businesses that can afford them, there is potential they will only be in wealthier areas.

SOCIAL STREETS

105

# RAAHGIRI DAY

*Gurgaon, India*

Known as the "Silicon Valley of India," Gurgaon in Haryana State south of Delhi is a hub for multinational companies and skyscrapers—and the traffic and pollution that fast growth brings. The streets are jammed with vehicles and there are almost no sidewalks or bike paths for non-motorized commuting.

Raahgiri began in November 2013 to raise awareness of the need for safe roads designed for people ("raah" means a path to reach a goal and "giri" refers to Gandhi's non-violent methods), much as Ciclovía began in Bogotá. The ultimate goal was to build a city with bicycle paths and pedestrian avenues interwoven through its urban landscape.

Every Sunday, from as early as 6 am (depending on the season and the heat), almost 10 miles of major streets throughout Gurgaon were entirely closed to automobiles in a loop route. One street on the route was different in that the central through lanes were closed for pedestrians and bicyclists while the outside access lanes remained open to the reduced Sunday traffic.

Raahgiri was started by a group of community nonprofits, in cooperation with the District administration and police. During the first year, over 350,000 people of all classes, castes and religions came together on the streets, walking, bicycling,

RIGHT: Photo by raahgiriday.com.

| 10' | 13' | 44' | 11' | 11' | 11' | 11' | 41' | 13' | 6' |
|---|---|---|---|---|---|---|---|---|---|
| Sidewalk | Service Lane | Median with Parking | Travel Lane | Travel Lane | Travel Lane | Travel Lane | Median with Parking | Service Lane | Sidewalk |

0' 2' 5'       15'

SHUSHANT MARG

ASHOKA MARG

SECTOR 30 MAIN ROAD

SOCIAL STREETS

0' 10' 20'     50'

playing, dancing, boarding, blading, playing games, doing zumba and yoga, and generally enjoying the festivities. Street vendors sold food, drink and trinkets.

On Raahgiri Day, streets were no longer just for getting from point A to point B, they *were* A and B. Over 44 percent of attendees were regular visitors to the street and 60 percent spent four hours or more at the event. Raahgiri proved so popular that the Haryana Urban Development Authority installed permanent cycle tracks for bicyclists in Gurgaon. In a survey of residents, 28 percent said that they had bought their own cycles after attending the Raahgiri Day, while 87 percent said that they now cycle or walk shorter distances rather than drive. And while 80 percent of merchants on Raahgiri streets were initially opposed, after one year 79 percent were in favor and reported sales increased by 29 percent.[9]

Word spread and now other cities including New Delhi, Ludhiana, Navi Mumbai and Bhopal have Raahgiri Days.

SOCIAL STREETS

109

**What Works** A great generator of social capital and civic pride. • The multi-way section allows the corridor to be closed to through traffic while still allowing local access. • Its success inspired over 200 km of new cycle lanes in the City. • Air quality has improved.

**Lessons Learned** Raahgiri Days require a lot of human intervention every week to close roads and clean up. • Success has come with accidents: a 14 percent increase in footfalls. • Some businesses still view it negatively; public communication needs to continue. • There is an impact on access to local businesses and residents along the non-multi-way boulevard.

# VIRTUALLY REAL, YEAH!

*Countrywide, USA*

On three blocks for eight weeks on Thursdays and Saturdays in the summer of 2014, Downtown Denver became an immersive street arcade. OhHeckYeah was three different interactive arcade games projected on huge video screens on street corners in the theater district.[10] Players in the street moved Denver's famous Blue Bear down from the mountains on screen by physically jumping in place, which made the bear jump over obstacles on screen ("Big Blue's Hood Slam"). They controlled characters to catch "good stuff" by moving their bodies from side to side ("Catchy") and worked as teams to align machine parts by running back and forth ("Tinker Bot").

Each game was specifically created for the event and about 40,000 people played that summer. Surrounding businesses offered karaoke, live music, theater and comedy, and food. To generate more interest, local improv comedians developed twitter feeds for the characters in the games, starting weeks before.

Meanwhile, hundreds of millions of people played "Ingress," and "Pokémon Go," massive multiplayer online games by Niantic Labs that brought Millennials back to the streets and interacting with other players. Location-tracking technology and Bluetooth devices let players scour the streets to capture

RIGHT: 16th Street and Champa Street, Denver. Photo by Brian Corrigan/OhHeckYeah.

SOCIAL STREETS

111

LEFT: 14th Street and Champa Street, Denver. Photo by Brian Corrigan/OhHeckYeah.

virtual creatures the game "placed" in various locations.[11]

And a bevy of online scavenger hunt apps let cities and individuals create hunts using clues about well-known and not-so-well-known spots around town. The City of Philadelphia worked with Scavify to create the New Americans tour, aimed at people becoming American citizens. Participants take photos, check in at tour locations and answer trivia questions about the locations, all while learning the answers to the questions on the citizenship test.

Klikaklu lets users create photo-based public hunts using a phone's camera and GPS. GooseChase is also photo-based, with a set of missions to accomplish (wacky or otherwise!), allowing unlimited numbers of teams. And StrayBoots has created self-guided tour/hunts in 70 cities and neighborhoods. Last clues often lead participants to a place to sit down and celebrate the game.[12]

Blending the physical and digital worlds breaks down barriers between strangers and pumps up interest in going downtown. OhHeckYeah developer Brian Corrigan says it works because people trust technology and they'll participate in programming that creates a shared experience—which creates social glue and integrates people into both the community and the physical space.[13]

**What Works**  Players enjoy the games and do engage with strangers on the street. • Surrounding businesses can get involved to increase foot traffic. • BIDs and arts groups helped finance the OhHeckYeah program.

**Lessons Learned**  Cities need quantifiable measures of success to justify the cost. • Games need to reflect the distinctiveness of place. • Social media needs independent publicity to reach a critical mass level of participation.

 Communities worldwide have found innovative methods to encourage people to gather on the street. Each of these case studies provides lessons learned, on which to build the best practices included at the end of this chapter. More information about these projects and programs is available on reStreets.org.

## GREEN LIGHT FOR MIDTOWN  *New York*

Few tourists, locals or office workers wanted to spend time in Times Square. The configuration of Broadway and Times Square caused some of the City's worst traffic back-ups and most hazardous pedestrian conditions in the City, with 562 crashes involving pedestrians and motor vehicles between 1995 and 2005.[14] The Green Light project reduced traffic congestion in the most counterintuitive way: take away space from cars, permanently close Broadway at Times Square and Herald Square to all cars, increase sidewalk space and crosswalks for pedestrians, increase crossing times, and add flexibility to close side streets at times. As a result, traffic injuries are down 63 percent, travel speeds have increased, and an amazing 74 percent of New Yorkers say Times Square has improved dramatically and they like to visit.[15]

## CICLOVÍA: A MOVEMENT  *Bogotá, Colombia*

Ciclovías (a mash-up of a Colombian slang word for bicycle, "cicla," and the word "via," thus, cycleways) are popping up all over the world. They began in 1974 in Bogotá as a response to congestion and pollution, and to overcome the bicycle's low status as a travel mode. Each Sunday and on public holidays from 7am until 2pm, specific main streets are blocked off to cars for bicyclists, runners, walkers and skaters. At the same time, stages are set up in City parks where aerobic and yoga instructors lead masses of people through various exercises, called Recrovía. About 2 million people join in (about 30 percent of Bogotá's population) on over 75 miles of car-free streets. There's now even an annual night ride, Ciclovía Nocturna.

### PARK(ING) DAY *Worldwide*

"Providing temporary public open space...one parking spot at a time," Park(ing) Day began in 2005 in San Francisco when a small group of people took over a parking spot for 2 hours (putting money in the meter) and converted it into a public park. They called attention to the lack of public open space in urban areas. The idea caught on worldwide. Now, on the third Friday in September, participants build parks, art installations, free health clinics, temporary urban farms, ecology demonstrations, political seminars and free bike repair shops. There's even been a wedding in one space. Some municipalities now have design guidelines for space "takeovers," although most simply agree to an unofficial day of no parking tickets for those spots.

### AT ONE WITH THE CREEK *Golden, Colorado*

The City of Golden, Colorado, needed to enhance the flood capacity of the Washington Avenue Bridge over Clear Creek, which runs right through the town. It took the opportunity to build a dramatic new bridge with generous sidewalks. It creates a dramatic gateway to the Downtown and celebrates Golden's mining history with black structural steel, red brick and native sandstone. The bridge incorporates large overlooks on both sides to view the creek and waterfront plaza below. The bridge decks include plenty of seating to encourage shoppers and visitors to linger and drivers to get out of their cars and enjoy the view.

### LITTLE ITALY REBOUNDS *San Diego, California*

In the 1970s, Interstate 5 was constructed through a thriving Little Italy community and 35 percent of the neighborhood was destroyed. The remaining area fell into blight for 20 years. A Community Benefit District and Business Improvement District run by the nonprofit Little Italy Association were key factors in the area's rebound.[16] They generate about $850,000 a year for streetscaping, decorations, events, maintenance and neighborhood security. Along with permanent seating, movable chairs are spread along the sidewalks, allowing people to customize an outdoor "living room." A highlight is Piazza Basilone with movable tables, chairs and a fountain that encourage lingering and shopping.[17, 18]

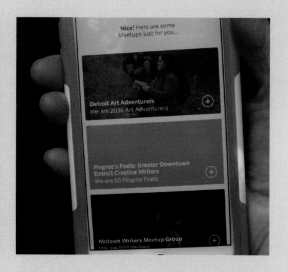

### A BUSY NIGHT OUT *Pittsburgh, Pennsylvania*

On every first Friday evening from May to October, the Garfield Night Market takes over two blocks on N. Pacific Avenue between Penn Avenue and Dearborn Street in this east end Pittsburgh neighborhood. Its goals are to foster Garfield's entrepreneurs, give families a place to spend a Friday night together and highlight Garfield's creativity and energy. Vendors include urban farms, arts and crafts, and food. It links experienced vendors with first-time neighborhood vendors to share best practices and boost the fledgling businesses. The Night Market also links with nearby Penn Avenue Unblurred, when the Penn Avenue Arts District opens for exploration by adults and children, showcasing a variety of artwork and free performances (that's year round).[19]

### SARDANA DANCES *Catalunya, Spain*

On Saturdays and Sundays in Catalunya, groups of residents come together and dance in the street and plazas. They're dancing the Sardana, a slow-motion group dance that looks deceptively simple. Dancers and musicians of all ages and backgrounds come to the street, place their belongings on the ground in the middle of the circle, hold hands with raised arms and follow a leader who leads the movements and timing. The dance can go on for hours, with people coming and going as they please. It had been banned during the rule of Francisco Franco (along with the Catalán language) because it is such a strong symbol of Catalán unity and independence. Where do they dance? There are formal Sardana at festivals, but the authentic dances occur at "hot spots" around town that locals just simply know about.

### THE ONLINE BECOMES REAL *Micro-communities*

The neighborly chats over the fence that had seemed to disappear, popped up online. And now, they're re-entering the physical world. Online forums such as Meetup.com help people meet other groups of people in their neighborhood to do everything from joining them for hikes and happy hours or learning R language. It says it's all about meeting online, then interacting with people in person. NextDoor.com creates online neighborhoods that match your actual neighborhood, and only those in the neighborhood can join that specific group. Typical postings are advertising community meetings, organizing a block party, a discussion about what's happening to the building on the next corner, a found set of keys and recommendations about a great handyman or window washer. There are many more online neighborhoods—at your fingertips.

LEFT: Photo by Garfield Night Market.   CENTER: Photo by SABET. "Sardana2." Licensed under Creative Commons 2.0.   RIGHT: Photo by Catherine Courtenaye/MIG, Inc.

### A WALK WITH ART  *Lyons, Colorado*

The historic Main Street in Downtown Lyons sorely needed some love and attention. The City reduced the travel lanes to two, which allowed for much wider sidewalks and a more pedestrian-friendly environment. In addition to spaces for outdoor dining and natural benches for sitting and chatting, the City incorporated bold and unexpected art elements throughout the two blocks. The art is designed to be touchable and even climbable, encouraging people of all ages to linger and return to enjoy the Downtown. Plus Downtown got an economic boost, increasing sales tax revenue by 10 percent in the first year after construction.

### HAVE A SEAT  *Abrantes, Portugal*

DomestiCITY prompted the residents of Abrantes to slow down and take a load off. The art installation won a Portuguese television channel's "urban intervention competition." The artists asked people for unwanted furniture and repaired, sanded and repainted about 60 chairs, writing desks, tables and stools with a multicolored palette. They arranged the furniture on the streets to create urban living rooms, encouraging talking, writing and drawing. To stimulate conversation, they posted helpful words on the sides of buildings and built a mailbox where residents can deposit more discussion topics for future "guests" who come to the living room.

### HOWDY, NEIGHBOR!  *Minneapolis, Minnesota*

Sidewalks are public realm and front yards are not. Or are they? So much of our experience walking the sidewalks of our communities is shaped by how the privately owned structures interact with our public realm. The Friendly Fronts initiative helps people turn their front yards into inviting, approachable gathering places—rethinking what it means to be neighborly. The Front Yard Placemaking Toolkit [20] offers ways to link front yards with the street. Among the ideas are seating areas where neighbors can watch kids play, fire pits, replacing tall privacy fences with shorter border features, installing a panel for showing "movies on the porch," adding inviting gateways and pathways, and transforming boulevards by placing seating near trees.

Seating, art, trees and shade-providing elements allow people to feel comfortable, stop, pause and gather. Adding elements like retractable bollards, multiuse seating, stages and a power supply can transform a space into an area that encourages people to play music, sing and dance. And wi-fi can bring in new technologies.

## Art

Interpretive and engaging art can reflect the neighborhood, its history and the people who live there and provide opportunities for learning. It also be functional.

## Banners

Hung at major intersections and on building, banners promote events to the community.

## Lighting

Lighting is important for nighttime visibility and a sense of security; it can also enhance a location's festive mood or character.

## Parking

Bike parking onsite and auto parking offsite (with shuttle service) can encourage alternate travel modes.

## Paving/painting

A variety of paving types and permanent or temporary paints can differentiate areas from roadway paving, provide safety surfacing, help with street calming and provide visual interest.

## Performance spaces

Permanent or temporary stages encourage both spontaneous and programmed music and street performances.

## Temporary landscape barriers

Permanent or temporary, planted screens, temporary fences, raised planter boxes and retractable bollards provide separation among street activities and protect landscaping.

## Temporary traffic blocks

Sawhorses, retractable bollards and movable planter boxes or containers can cordon off areas and block traffic if the street is to be closed at times.

## Trash and recycling receptacles

Receptacles are essential for maintaining cleanliness and an attractive public space. During an event, both the numbers and sizes of the receptacles should be greatly increased.

## Trees and vegetation

Trees and vegetation help provide a human scale and can be placed to calm traffic, while providing shade and habitat.

### Directional signage

Signage will direct attendees about where to go so they can see or do their preferred activities.

### Drinking water

For people and pets, water can be provided through drinking fountains, water bottle filling stations, etc.

### Flexible lanes

Flexible travel lanes, parking lanes and pedestrian paths help increase available gathering space, as well as manage and direct both event attendees and those trying to get around the event.

### Furniture

Fixed and movable tables and seating, made of materials that are durable and require minimal maintenance, provide comfortable surfaces.

### Power sources

Electrical outlets support a variety of social activities such as sound systems, generators and lights, as well as recharging laptops, cell phones and mobile reading devices.

### Public restrooms

This basic amenity can encourage people to gather and stay for extended periods of time and is critical to reduce the impact of crowds on the surrounding neighborhood.

### Staging and storage

Open areas for loading/ unloading and constructing elements will lessen impact on existing businesses. Storage onsite will help with set up, especially for multi-day events.

### Structures

Arbors, pergolas, canopies and tents provide protection from the elements and function as gathering spots; booths and tables offer spaces for displaying goods and information.

### Water source

Water is needed for cleaning and maintaining the physical environment.

### Wi-fi

Technology opens up new ways of socializing on the street and makes it easy to locate instant information about social and cultural events, discover the history of a place and post photos from an event.

# CREATING A SOCIAL GATHERING STREET

Just a basic level of infrastructure such as seat walls of different heights along a sidewalk, fences with nooks for sitting, and movable tables and chairs can support informal interactions.

However, to attract people who would not normally come to the street to experience it as a social space, spaces need a higher level of street infrastructure and structures such as stages and permanent or temporal marked spaces. Combining a diversity of "sticky" elements will attract people's attention—often because they are unexpected— and encourage people to linger in the space.

Streets should provide the infrastructure and framework for varied and ever-changing activities and events for people of all ages and abilities. The street should include spaces that accommodate different scales of human interaction, including intimate settings for families and friends, informal interactions between individuals, areas for people with pets and spots for small and large group meet ups. The social experience can be woven into the function of the street so it becomes a natural and common occurrence. William Whyte describes many physical elements beautifully in *The Social Life of Small Urban Spaces*.[21] Here are more ideas to consider.

## Optimize streets for gathering

(1) Lower the speed limit for traffic to no more than 20 mph at all times.

(2) Encourage speed limits of 20 mph or less to minimize impacts of traffic on the social character of the street.

(3) Limit and control the types of heavy vehicles on the street. For example, manage truck traffic and control deliveries and service vehicles by setting restrictions on location and time of use.

(4) Ensure that the space for automobiles is not more than 50 percent of the right-of-way. Where possible, encourage no more than three lanes that are 10- to 11-feet wide.

(5) Use street-calming elements, such as trees, raised intersections, special paving and bulb outs.

## Promote a "pedestrian-first" character

**1** Design wide enough sidewalks to allow pedestrian movement and gathering to happen simultaneously.

**2** Create flush or level streets without curbs and gutters to create a seamless space for larger gatherings.

**3** Use sidewalk reflective paving materials or colors in parts of the roadway, such as the parking lane, to extend the pedestrian-friendly character of the street.

**4** Integrate adjacent uses with the sidewalk articulation like seating near cafes.

**5** Incorporate vertical elements (lighting, shade structures, trees and planting) to provide an intimate human scale to the street.

## Create flexible spaces

**1** Implement flexible travel lanes that can be used differently during different times, e.g., a couple of parking spaces can become a temporary outdoor gathering space one day a week or a permanent parklet.

**2** Incorporate movable features, such as seating, container planting, screens, bollards, etc., that can be used to change the size and scale of spaces and for temporary barriers when streets are closed to traffic.

**3** Provide seating areas for gathering at already active places, such as bus stops.

**4** Choose elements that allow for change in usage depending on time of day or year, such as temporary shade structures, lighting, etc.

**5** Reduce the number and width of travel lanes to provide more space for non-automobile usage of the street, either permanently or temporary.

## Design for gathering and human interaction

**1** Provide outdoor living rooms to accommodate groups of various sizes and ages.

**2** Provide seating at regular intervals on the street. Seating should include benches, chairs, seatwalls, or a variety of other "perches."

**3** Offer movable seating that allows people to create their own outdoor living rooms.

**4** Provide comfort that responds to climatic conditions and provides shelter from elements including wind and rain.

**5** Provide quiet places to gather, such as street gardens with plantings and benches set back from the roadway.

**6** Install shared community resources such as libraries and community notice boards for announcements of community events and services.

**7** Provide idea walls for people to share art, poetry and stories.

**8** Set up speaker corners that encourage public speaking, debate and discussion.

**9** Provide opportunities for play for all ages such as chess boards and musical instruments (see Chapter 6, Play Streets).

**10** In addition to well-tested design concepts, test new ideas such as pianos, book clubs, etc., to encourage serendipitous gathering.

## Provide gathering spaces for all

**1** Incorporate a variety of seating to accommodate a range of physical abilities, and companion seating that enables wheelchair users to sit next to friends or family members.

**2** Ensure permanent ADA accessible seating every quarter mile.

**3** Place all signs, shade elements (such as umbrellas or trees) or other features 80 inches or higher above ground so they don't pose a hazard.

**4** Avoid any protrusions into pedestrian travel ways that are higher than 27 inches so someone with a visual impairment can detect them with a cane.

**5** Ensure that all pedestrian travel surfaces are firm, stable and slip-resistant.

LEFT: West Capitol Avenue, West Sacramento. Project design and photo by MIG, Inc.

## Strengthen community identity

(1) Install interpretive art that celebrates community life and highlights local history or ecology.

(2) Create a distinct focal point, such as a large gateway sculpture or a water feature that provides an identity and meeting place for the neighborhood.

(3) Organize collaborative art events, such as mural painting, that allow the community to participate.

(4) Place playful and interactive art in unexpected places that relate to the environment, (perhaps either larger than life or in miniature) to encourage children to be equal users of the street.

## Select streets for special events

**1** Select streets that offer easy sight lines for police and event security staff, and can accommodate ADA needs; ensure a minimum 5-foot wide clear pedestrian travel lane for wheelchairs.

**2** Select streets with minimal slopes along the event route (except for ciclovías).

**3** Select streets that have appropriate connectivity for multiple modes of transportation, including cars, mass transit, biking and walking.

**4** Encourage non-auto access for large events and free shuttle service from nearby transit stops and parking garages. Locate ample bicycle parking at key nodes. Partner with local bike advocacy groups to provide secure parking.

**5** Ensure that streets have emergency access, especially when closing the street temporarily, either within a street traffic lane or along the sidewalk.

**6** Designate streets that don't have special materials (sidewalk paving, special lights) that could be damaged by heavy foot traffic and moving equipment.

**7** Ensure that temporary loss of street or neighborhood connectivity is balanced by the benefits of creating large, well-used social spaces that bring together people from all walks of life.

## Provide infrastructure for special events and street closures

(1) Provide convenient ways to temporarily close streets or parking lanes through retractable bollards, movable planters, etc.

(2) Provide essential portable elements such as seating, restrooms, water stations, etc. Where possible, partner with adjoining businesses for temporary use of restrooms for small events.

(3) Provide elements that facilitate the event, such as performance stage, sound system, trash and recycling receptacles, etc.

(4) Design for temporary or permanent access to power for electrical systems. Design new "event" streets with power outlets in pedestrian lights and seating walls, and with water sources and systems for disposing of graywater.

(5) Provide directional signage and wayfinding both for attendees and for autos trying to avoid the event.

(6) Develop a citywide program for closing entire sections of streets temporarily or permanently, and citywide policy and permitting guidelines so the street can be used for a diversity of gatherings through street closures, event permits, etc.

(7) Communicate with businesses and residences along the route about altered access and alternatives.

(8) Test out new street ideas ,such as protected bike lanes, during temporary events.

SOCIAL STREETS

129

# Use the "virtual" to promote the physical reality

**1** Ensure that there are communications plans to publicize events, using both traditional and new media.

**2** Develop a website for ongoing or large events.

**3** Provide online review sites for public spaces that promote amenities, events and programming.

**4** Promote online sharing forums to encourage social contact among neighbors that can translate into meeting in person.

**5** Use social media to connect residents to opportunities for social events in the neighborhood and on the street.

**6** Provide free wi-fi and charging stations.

**7** Create online games such as treasure hunts and scavenger hunts that integrate with the street.

## Provide a human infrastructure

(1) Involve stakeholder groups from conception to construction and maintenance of special events and outdoor living rooms.

(2) Establish business improvement districts (BID) and/or neighborhood associations for continued financial support and maintenance.

(3) Encourage community members and BIDs to sponsor and maintain special art and furnishings.

(4) Determine the best sponsor for special events, such as local government or nonprofit organizations, and ensure that there is a responsible oversight group.

(5) Tap into a variety of funding sources, such as government agency sponsorship, grants, corporate sponsorships, as well as fees such as admissions, booth fees or parking/bike parking fees.

(6) Obtain or help groups obtain necessary permits and consider creating an "event permit package" to facilitate event creation.

(7) Identify staffing needs, including volunteer coordination, recruitment and supervision.

(8) Consider creating an event furniture kit including movable chairs and tables, umbrellas, shade structures, play elements and portable trees that groups can borrow.

(9) Provide training for staff and volunteers.

SOCIAL STREETS

131

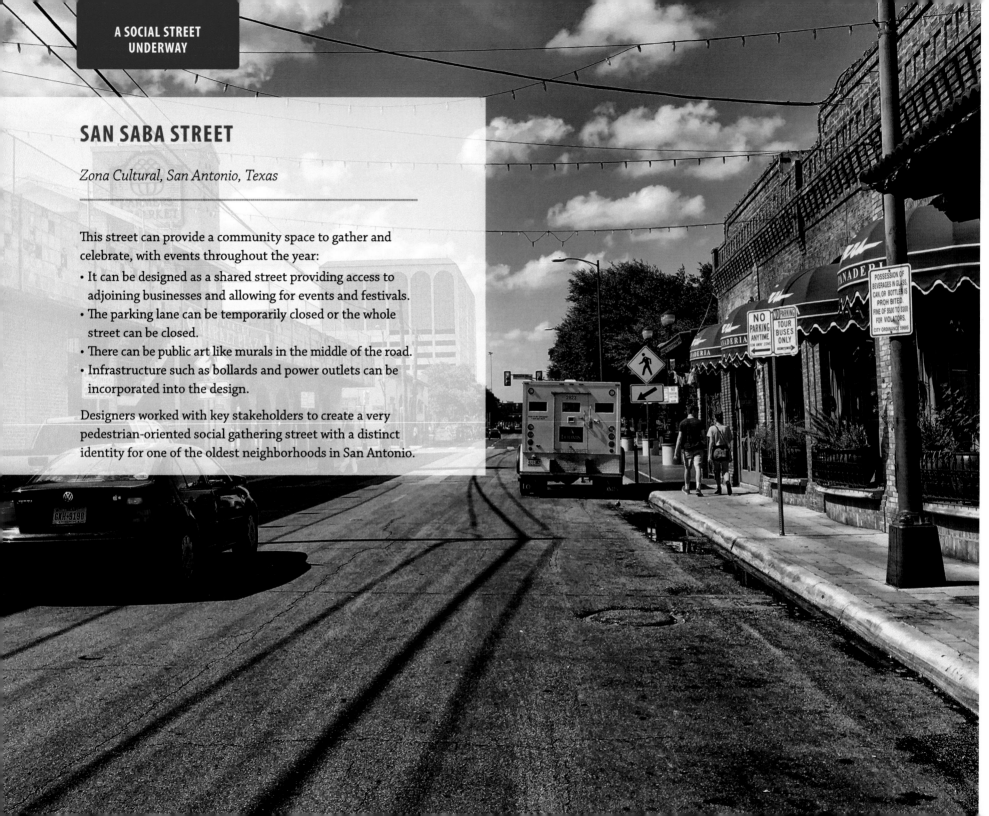

# SAN SABA STREET

*Zona Cultural, San Antonio, Texas*

This street can provide a community space to gather and celebrate, with events throughout the year:

- It can be designed as a shared street providing access to adjoining businesses and allowing for events and festivals.
- The parking lane can be temporarily closed or the whole street can be closed.
- There can be public art like murals in the middle of the road.
- Infrastructure such as bollards and power outlets can be incorporated into the design.

Designers worked with key stakeholders to create a very pedestrian-oriented social gathering street with a distinct identity for one of the oldest neighborhoods in San Antonio.

POSSESSION OF
BEVERAGES IN GLASS,
CAN, OR BOTTLE IS
PROHIBITED.
FINE OF $500 TO $200
FOR VIOLATORS.
CITY ORDINANCE 59885

# 5

## SHOP ON THE STREET

*Shopping Streets*

Blend one part entrepreneurial spirit with a dash of new technology and mix well with the street. The result: an elixir to enhance commerce and jobs—and the variety of people involved in them.

In the United States, commerce has usually been located in the private realm, inside stores or offices or other privately owned and operated spaces. And, with few exceptions, where commerce has entered the public realm, it has been relegated to a little slip of land on the sidewalk between buildings and the pedestrian travel way. This is the usual habitat of outdoor dining, sidewalk sales and newspaper vending machines. But expanding the concept of streets and the definition of commerce can encourage new types of businesses with new types of entrepreneurs—and more of them.

**WHY SHOP ON THE STREET?**

Including a variety of commerce types in a variety of areas creates opportunities for a diversity of entrepreneurs, from the fledgling business owner to well-established businesses. The advantage to adding both stand-alone and temporary commerce to the street is the barrier to entry (specifically funding) can be much lower than for a traditional brick-and-mortar business. It's a new way for those with entrepreneurial spirit but limited resources to participate in a growing economy.

This increased entrepreneurial energy helps all businesses increase their customer base: people are attracted to areas that they can experience as more than just a trip to the store. The result is an environment that hums with commercial activity and the promise of increased prosperity.

To lure shoppers out from behind their laptops and their online ordering, commercial districts need to provide a rich, experiential setting in which to shop—a place that is attractive, lively and creates a long-lasting positive memory beyond the shopping itself. That means providing more than just a few stores and stalls. Street design for commerce needs to include all the spaces *between* the stores, an entire area or district.

Many upgrades to the shopper's experience can be made within areas that are historically used for commerce, such as main streets, where the existing system of sidewalks, parking areas and private development helps create the necessary framework for active commerce.

However, cities can also capitalize on underutilized and "residual" spaces that are traditionally devoted to mobility. There are bits of land available within the street or public right-of-way, such as sidewalks, plazas, bulb outs, medians and even in parking and travel lanes on a temporary basis. For example, in some areas parking lanes might simply be for parking, while in other areas they might sometimes be for temporary retail carts, food vendors or farmers markets. And in places that can be readily accessed without cars, a traditional "parking" zone might be permanently converted to other uses.

Commerce can also be more than just selling and eating. Street performers, musicians, magicians, singers, dancers, painters and, yes, even mimes can be encouraged to come to the street with just a few streetscape changes. Bringing all types of commerce to all types of areas extends the life of the street beyond the traditional 9–6 shopping hours when many streets typically die. Good street design can support three main types of commerce:

- **Traditional commerce.** These types of activities support the commerce of adjacent brick-and-mortar businesses through product displays, open studios, outdoor dining and sidewalk sales. We are used to seeing these types of activities on the street.

- **Micro-liner retail.** These permanent businesses are independent of the adjoining establishments—and fit into niches in the building wall or in permanent kiosks. They include business such as newspaper kiosks, fruit and vegetable stands, specialty clothing and accessories outlets and flower shops.

SHOPPING STREETS

**137**

• **Temporary/mobile commerce.** These activities are not physically integrated with the private realm and can move around to find their best audiences. This includes food carts, food trucks, horse-drawn carriage or cart rides, open studios, demonstration displays and even light manufacturing right on the spot.

Cities are hubs of commercial innovation, drawing entrepreneurial individuals from all social strata. An economically healthy area in the city attracts more residents and investment, while economically weak or distressed areas struggle with crime and disinvestment. Healthy commerce can be an engine for job creation and provide funding for maintenance, libraries, parks, social services and other community priorities.

## GOALS

Streets designed for commerce should provide safe and easily accessible places that contribute to the overall vitality and ambiance of the street, aiming to:

• Maximize economic development of varying types (single owner/operator, small businesses, companies) and scales (single food cart, food truck, permanent kiosk).

• Create an identity and sense of place that strengthens the commercial area as a singular destination.

• Ensure that vendors can rely on steady, year-round (multi-seasonal) business.

LEFT: Manhattan. Photo by MIG, Inc.

**ACTIVITIES ON A SHOPPING STREET**

Streets that include commerce should be designed to host a diversity of activities that use the street, both during the day and the night. Uses might also change on different days of the week and during different seasons.

# 16TH STREET MALL
*Denver, Colorado*

The mile-high City of Denver boasts a mile-long mall that's been called the premier pedestrian environment in the Rocky Mountain Region. Built in 1982, it's a tree-lined promenade filled with shops and offices, outdoor cafes, street carts, kiosks, trees and public art—with ample space for sitting and performance events.[1]

The original Mall had an 80-foot wide public right-of-way. The central 7 blocks are symmetrical; a large central median provides space for vending carts and kiosk businesses and includes a double row of trees and pedestrian lights. The three blocks on either end are asymmetrical, with a 35-foot wide sidewalk on one side and a narrow median.[2]

A main feature is a granite paver system that mimics the skin of a western Diamondback rattlesnake and runs the entire street. Despite initial hesitancy about installing anything not anchored in place, movable seating is a key attraction, allowing groups to form at will. Planters and trash receptacles located in the median and on sidewalks are also movable.

In addition to about 300 brick-and-mortar restaurants and retailers, in 2015 the Mall

LEFT: 16th Street, Denver. Photo by VISIT DENVER.

RIGHT: 16th Street, Denver. Photo by VISIT DENVER.

SHOPPING STREETS

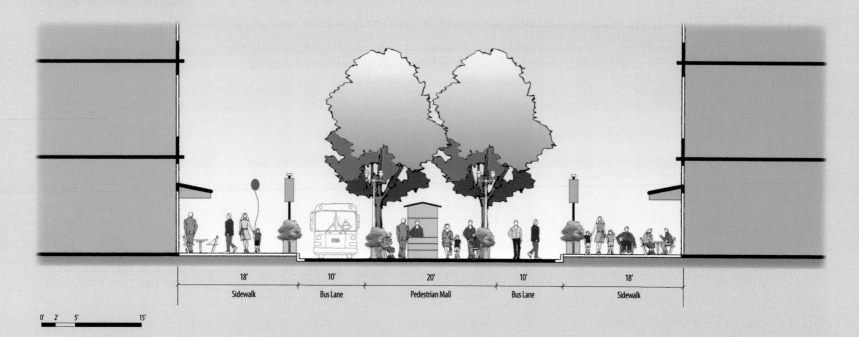

| 18' | 10' | 20' | 10' | 18' |
|---|---|---|---|---|
| Sidewalk | Bus Lane | Pedestrian Mall | Bus Lane | Sidewalk |

0'  2'  5'          15'

16TH STREET        16TH STREET        16TH STREET

ALLEY

ALLEY

CHAMPA STREET

SOUTH STREET

0'  10'  20'        50'

was home to 15 street cart vendors, 3 semi-permanent kiosks, 6 seasonal kiosks, 42 sidewalk cafes, 8 separate horse and carriage ride companies and hosts about 65 events, fairs and markets every year.[3]

Free hybrid electric-LNG shuttle buses, operated by the Regional Transit District, stop on every corner and nearly 50,000 people use them on an average weekday. Shuttles run 20 hours a day, and are only 90 seconds apart during peak periods (morning commute, lunch time and evening commute). The shuttle links with light rail stations, the newly rejunvenated Union Terminal, express bus terminals and local bus routes—no need for cars at all.

The City implemented zoning and urban design guidelines after the Mall was built that helped preserve impressive view corridors and encourage public art, including a "sunlight ordinance" to enforce height restrictions. Strategic investments by the Denver Urban Renewal Authority encouraged preservation of facades of historic buildings and ground floor retail in new development. The Mall is maintained by the Downtown Denver Business Improvement District.

RIGHT: 16th Street, Denver. Photo by VISIT DENVER.

SHOPPING STREETS

143

**What Works** High-quality design and materials create a unique sense of place and a destination for locals and tourists. • Commerce opportunities are very diverse. • The BID, whose primary focus is the Mall, maintains it so well that incidents of theft or vandalism of street furniture are very rare. • The free shuttle offers easy, convenient access.

**Lessons Learned** The granite pavers require more maintenance than expected. • Food vendors must be close to intersections so they can be easily removed at day's end. • The median can attract the homeless and groups of youths who may intimidate others. • The Mall's design and frequency of shuttles encourages movement, but not window shopping or large gatherings. • Efforts are being made to improve the Mall design and overall functionality.

# JL MALIOBORO STREET
*Yogyakarta, Indonesia*

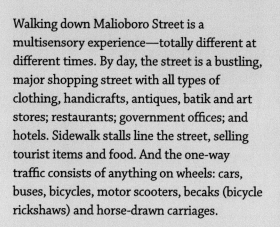

Walking down Malioboro Street is a multisensory experience—totally different at different times. By day, the street is a bustling, major shopping street with all types of clothing, handicrafts, antiques, batik and art stores; restaurants; government offices; and hotels. Sidewalk stalls line the street, selling tourist items and food. And the one-way traffic consists of anything on wheels: cars, buses, bicycles, motor scooters, becaks (bicycle rickshaws) and horse-drawn carriages.

The street changes completely at night, after the stores and offices close and the hot, humid day has cooled. Seemingly out of nowhere "lesehan" pop up—portable kitchens with tent covers—and the tempting smells of spices, meats, jackfruit, coconuts and soups waft over the street. The kitchens convert the blank building walls into busy commercial zones. After the daytime street vendors leave, those spots are covered in straw mats and tables for customers. And then come musicians playing traditional Javanese instruments like the gamelan, the pantomime acts, the famous Javanese puppet shows, and the singers and dancers. Roving "pikulan" vendors appear, holding two bundles connected by a stick across their shoulders;

SHOPPING STREETS

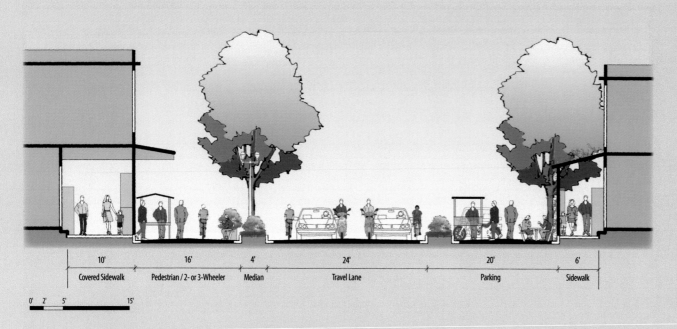

| 10' | 16' | 4' | 24' | 20' | 6' |
|---|---|---|---|---|---|
| Covered Sidewalk | Pedestrian / 2- or 3-Wheeler | Median | Travel Lane | Parking | Sidewalk |

0'  2'  5'                    15'

SHOPPING STREETS

146

JL. BUMIJO TENGAH

JL. MALIOBORO STREET

JL. MALIOBORO STREET

JL. GOWANGAN LOR

0'  10'  20'        50'

one side might be a gas stove and wok with soup, the other serving bowls.

The design of the street allows for re-purposing the non-auto traffic lanes so commerce expands at night but traffic still flows through. The City integrated well-designed bike lanes and bike boxes—painted green at intersections in front of where cars must stop—reserved for bicyclists. They've also installed special paving materials to denote pedestrian areas, well-marked crosswalks at regular intervals and pedestrian refuge areas so pedestrians can cross the street despite the onslaught of traffic. The sidewalks are generously sized and the medians separating different modes of travel are raised and articulated with bollards, trees, decorative lights, signage and sculptures. The entire street is designed to encourage strolling and pausing at shops, meeting friends and enjoying life on the street almost 24 hours a day.

SHOPPING STREETS

147

**What Works** Daytime commerce seamlessly transitions to nighttime commerce. • Flexible street design allows for easy partial street closure without hindering through traffic. • Small, entrepreneurial shops, restaurants and performers can use the same public right-of-way as high-end shops; they don't need expensive brick and mortar.

**Lessons Learned** The overflow of outdoor commerce can hinder ADA access and vulnerable users. • Sometimes high traffic noise detracts from music and theater performances. • Too much of a good thing: the street's high popularity deters some locals from coming in the evening.

 Communities worldwide have found innovative solutions to finding space for commerce on the street. Each of them provides lessons learned, on which to build the best practices included at the end of this chapter. More information about these projects and programs is available on www.reStreets.org.

### THE BOUQUINISTES *Paris, France*

Now a fixture in Paris, the Bouquinistes booksellers ply their trade along large sections along the banks of the Seine. Each is licensed by the City and given four permanently placed metal boxes that are about 6 feet long by 3 feet wide. When opened, the top edge of the box is about 6 feet above ground. Bouquinistes pay rent for the stone on which the boxes sit (around $150 a year). They also pay all maintenance costs, including the required *vert wagon* paint (the green color of old train cars). The most coveted spots are awarded based on seniority; the wait list is 8 years. With such little overhead, prices for books, pamphlets and other printed materials are usually cheaper than in shops and a favorite with tourists.

### PUBLIC DINING *Mountain View, California*

Mountain View, in the heart of Silicon Valley, felt indiscernible from the rest of the urban area. So the City revitalized the Downtown, including its main thoroughfare, Castro Street. It was 90 feet wide with 4 lanes of traffic and 10-foot sidewalks—just slivers of space for pedestrians. The new design reduces traffic to three lanes, resulting in an asphalt crossing of just 34 feet. While the 10-foot sidewalks remain, the City also created flexible zones in the public realm that can be used for parking or for outdoor dining, taking up to 32 spaces. Businesses must apply annually to use the zone and must follow design guidelines for all furniture, planters, landscaping, and even the dishes and utensils used in the zone.[4, 5]

### HEROES DINING DECK *Mobile, Alabama*

Borrowing from the "parklet" concept, Heroes Sports Bar and Grille expanded its dining area into the public realm in 2004, claiming two on-street parking spaces for an outdoor seating deck. The City's mayor was looking for innovative ways to reenergize the Downtown area and thought this could open up gathering areas—and generate tax revenue. Heroes currently has the only public realm deck in the City, although other merchants are considering it.[6] Heroes' deck only seats patrons of the restaurant during business hours, but strollers often stop and chat over the rails with friends who are dining.

### SAI YEUNG CHOI STREET SOUTH *Mong Kok, Hong Kong*

Everyone looking for electronics in Hong Kong is drawn to Sai Yeung Choi Street South with its concentration of electronic shops spilling out onto the sidewalks, bookstores above and dizzying displays of neon. It was built on watercress fields that eventually gave way to the highrises of today. Sai yeung choi means watercress, although the street is nicknamed Electronic Street—every name brand electronic store has a branch or two there. Portions are closed off to vehicles at night when the street comes alive with singing, kung fu shows, magic performances and dancing. Just about everything is sold there, from food to shoes to flowers. The only thing that might not be available is watercress!

### FOOD TRUCKS *Bozeman, Montana*

Sometimes no regulation at all works best. At about 9 pm on Fridays and Saturdays, food trucks, including Tumbleweeds, roll into Downtown Bozeman to serve the late night bar crowds. Tumbleweeds owner Jay Blaske serves gourmet tacos in a variety of styles, from American BBQ to Korean.[7] He says the "unwritten rule" is food trucks stay out of Downtown when restaurant kitchens are open, going instead to special events, corporate offices and farmers markets.[8] But restaurant bars often stay open late and food trucks help sell more drinks. The trucks use social media to alert customers to where they'll be at specific times. Opening a food truck in Bozeman simply requires a business license and health department inspection. That's it! Everything else is on the honor system and working just fine.

Movable furniture and carts and permanent stands encourage cooking, dining, buying and selling. Adding elements like power and water sources and festive lighting strengthens the incentive for people to more regularly participate in street activities at different times of day.

### Access and parking

Needed for deliveries, trucks, bicycles and autos, access can be strategically placed along the commercial street.

### Bike corrals

Safe bike parking attracts crowds and can be sponsored by local businesses to maintain them.

### Kiosks

Small or large kiosks for anything from jewelry to flowers to coffee can animate sidewalks and medians. They can be locked at night.

### Lighting

Traditional lighting is important for nighttime visibility and a sense of security. Festive lighting can also enhance a location's mood or character, especially during holidays.

### Liner stands

Temporary or permanent lockable liner stands can be designed as part of a building structure (liner retail) or creatively added along an inactive or blank edge of a building.

### Movable carts

Carts carry everything a business owner needs and can move with the seasons and change with the market.

### Structures

Arbors, pergolas, canopies and tents protect both vendors and the public from the elements and function as gathering spots.

### Temporary traffic blocks

Retractable bollards and movable planter boxes or containers can block traffic if the street is to be closed at times.

### Trash and recycling receptacles

Receptacles are essential for maintaining cleanliness and an attractive public space.

### Trees and vegetation

Shade for people and habitat for birds and animals is essential.

## Charging stations

Located at key nodes and gathering spaces, they can be combined with signage, wayfinding and advertising.

## Drinking water

For people and pets, water can be provided through drinking fountains, water bottle filling stations, etc.

## Furniture

Fixed and movable tables and seating, made of materials that are durable and require minimal maintenance, provide comfortable surfaces for eating, meeting and working.

## Infrastructure

Grease traps, sewer drains, and stormwater catchment areas handle the refuse created by food production and other commerce.

## Paving

A variety of paving types can differentiate shopping areas from roadways, designate areas for commerce and walking, and help with street calming.

## Power sources

Power from standard electrical outlets or onsite solar panels is essential for a range of needs, such as speakers, cooking equipment, computers, etc.

## Public restrooms

On commercial streets, this basic amenity can encourage people to gather and stay for extended periods of time.

## Signage

Visually identify places where commerce is located, perhaps by theme or type.

## Water source

Many vendors will need water for cleaning and maintaining the physical environment, cooking, hand washing and other business uses.

## Wi-fi

Connectivity allows customers to get information about businesses in the area and allows businesses to update product ads, "tweet" announcements and send emails to customers.

# CREATING A SHOPPING STREET

A well-designed combination of elements, amenities and programs are essential for streets designed for commerce. Some best practices support the commercial activities—at different times of day, days of the week and seasons—and some provide a comfortable and safe environment for customers. These best practices will help integrate street-based traditional permanent commerce, temporary and mobile commerce and micro-commerce into both existing commercial areas and areas that currently do not have commercial activities.

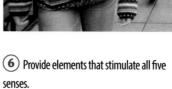

LEFT: Photo by Pat Guiney, "Paris Cafe." Licensed under Creative Commons 2.0.    RIGHT: Winslow Way, Bainbridge Island, Washington. Project design and photo by MIG, Inc.

# Ensure comfort and convenience

**①** Limit vehicular speed to 25 mph or less. Design for no more than 15 mph at all times on shared-use streets.

**②** Ensure that all commerce areas provide protection from the elements. Provide ample shade trees, awnings or other overhead elements.

**③** Maintain sight lines and clear visual paths to encourage strolling and discovering new sites and vendors.

**④** Provide seating at regular intervals and according to specific user needs along the street. Seating can include benches, chairs and seatwalls, as well as companion seating that enables wheelchair users to sit next to friends or family members.

**⑤** In addition to seating related to specific business areas, incorporate permanent and movable seating along the travel way to provide places to rest or "people watch."

**⑥** Provide elements that stimulate all five senses.

**⑦** To ensure that the street has an overarching pedestrian scale and character, encourage no more than two vehicle travel lanes in each direction, with each lane being a maximum width of 10 feet.

**⑧** Carefully locate site furnishings so that they function effectively, but avoid a cluttered look.

**⑨** Provide transit stops at least every ¼ mile, and include shelter and seating for waiting passengers.

**⑩** If the street is long, consider operating a shuttle service to get people back to cars or to transit.

RIGHT: Castro Street, Mountain View, California. Photo by MIG, Inc.

## Allow flexible use zones

**1** Establish a flexible use zone between the necessary travel lane and pedestrian path. Use materials or colors to both distinguish the flexible use zone from the vehicular travel way and connect it to the pedestrian area. These zones could include the parking lane, an adjoining travel lane that is closed during off-peak periods and a wide median in shared-use streets.

**2** Ensure that the flexible use zone can accommodate the size of a typical food truck or vendor cart as well as a variety of "two-top" dining tables with chairs—usually 6 feet wide or more.

**3** When flexible use zones are used for outdoor dining, provide an attractive barrier between the vehicular travel lanes and the pedestrian walkway. Barriers should be a minimum of 18 inches wide and from 3 feet to a maximum of 4 feet tall. Consider using movable planters or other sculptural elements as barriers.

**4** Encourage street festivals or farmers markets that temporarily utilize the parking lane or vehicular way as a commerce zone.

**5** Use the flexible zone to create one or two larger plazas, to allow performances, smaller festivals or vendor cart areas.

**6** Maintain some on-street parking spaces in the flexible lane to support adjoining businesses and calm traffic.

**7** Allow loading and unloading of commercially related vehicles to occur in the parking lane during designated off-peak hours.

## Encourage day and evening micro retail on the same street

**1** Depending on the space available, deploy a range of standard kiosk sizes from about 3 feet x 5 feet to 8 feet x 10 feet. These kiosk structures can expand when open.

**2** When locating micro retail, ensure that a continuous 5-foot to 8-foot ADA-compliant pedestrian access is provided along the sidewalk at all times.

**3** Provide temporary liner retail along blank walls, along unfriendly parking lots and structures or construction fences.

**4** Provide permanent micro retail opportunities in new buildings that cannot afford a pedestrian-friendly edge.

**5** Ensure that micro retail structures provide an attractive street presence even when businesses are closed. Incorporate art and lighting to activate the pedestrian area.

**6** Consider the use of shipping containers for single- and multistory micro retail opportunities.

**7** Position kiosks or stands to avoid blocking the view of traditional commerce areas such as market halls or retail spaces.

SHOPPING STREETS

**157**

## Encourage day and evening temporal commerce on the same street

**1** Locate temporal commerce opportunities on major local and tourist-serving commercial corridors with high daytime uses such as offices and stores that close in the evening.

**2** Design streets so some portion (sidewalk, parking lane, travel lanes) can be used for temporal commerce. Prioritize locations along passive or inactive building sides and open space edges along the street.

**3** Design architectural elements such as arcades and colonnades to host temporal commerce opportunities. Similarly, elements such as canopies that minimize heat gain can be extended and serve as tent structures for outdoor uses at night.

**4** Provide supporting infrastructure within the street right-of-way, such as water and electrical connections and retractable bollards.

**5** Provide flexible furniture that can serve different purposes—seat walls can become elevated podiums for outdoor performances, lights become vertical supports for canopies, etc.

**6** Reorganize portions of the street to transform to other uses at other times, for example, the sidewalk in front of a closed office can be used in the evening for busking, outdoor yoga, preparing and selling food.

**7** Provide a 12-foot contiguous pathway for emergency access on closed streets and ensure nothing impairs access to streets and closed buildings.

**8** As with micro retail, ensure a clear ADA-compliant 5- to 8-foot path of travel.

**9** Provide good light at night, with street- and pedestrian-level lighting of minimum 1 foot candle.

SHOPPING STREETS

*159*

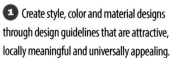

## Develop a unique identity

❶ Create style, color and material designs through design guidelines that are attractive, locally meaningful and universally appealing.

❷ Create a neighborhood identity by drawing on a local industry (current or historic), an area theme or another cultural or historical element.

❸ Incorporate a distinctive furnishing and planting palette that reflects the desired street character and image, and is visually attractive year round.

❹ Engage local artists to develop signature elements such as murals, sculptures or site furnishings that reflect local history and culture.

❺ Where possible, integrate art as part of functional features—benches, lighting, walls, kiosks, space dividers, planters and shade structures can all be works of art.

⑥ Incorporate bus shelters that can provide a wide variety of retail opportunities.

LEFT, RIGHT: India Street, Little Italy, San Diego. Photos by Catherine Courtenaye/MIG, Inc.

LEFT: Grant Street, entry to San Francisco Chinatown. Photo by Daniel Hartwig. Licensed under Creative Commons 2.0  RIGHT: Orchard Road, Singapore. Photo by MIG, Inc.

## Promote individual commercial areas

**1** Develop an attractive brand for the street or neighborhood, giving potential customers a sense of the street character, as well as the available goods or services.

**2** Incorporate the street or neighborhood brand and character into gateways and street signs.

**3** Provide a web page for the street or area, including the opportunity for small entrepreneurs to have an individual page on the site and/or a link to their own website.

**4** Maximize social media such as Twitter and Facebook to advertise both existing and new locations of mobile carts.

**5** When possible, consider unique marketing and advertising campaigns for each commercial area to promote services and wares.

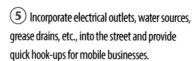

LEFT: SW Fifth Avenue, Portland, Oregon. Photo by Steve Leathers/MIG, Inc.   RIGHT: Nicollet Avenue, Minneapolis. Photo by MIG, Inc.

# Balance investment and maintenance costs

**1** Incorporate a maintenance budget for high pedestrian traffic areas.

**2** Use durable materials that show minimal wear with repeated and heavy use, such as concrete and stone.

**3** Emphasize finishes that require minimal maintenance.

**4** Consider the use of structural soil or other new technologies to provide a suitable environment for healthy tree root growth and to minimize damage to adjacent paving.

**5** Incorporate electrical outlets, water sources, grease drains, etc., into the street and provide quick hook-ups for mobile businesses.

**6** Ensure that flexible use zones and pedestrian travel ways are kept clean and free of trash or debris.

**7** Require all food vendors to keep the area within 25 feet of their space clean and litter- and garbage-free.

**8** Ensure that all tables, benches and other sitting areas are cleaned regularly and are attractive to users.

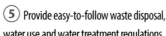

## Enact supporting policies

**(1)** Encourage business improvement districts (BIDs) to strengthen safety, maintenance, marketing and programming activities.

**(2)** Allow food cart vendors to maintain a mobile business classification, while also providing them with consistent locations from which to operate so that customers can find them easily.

**(3)** Provide mobile vendors with technical assistance regarding permitting and utility connections to help ease the start-up process.

**(4)** Implement a convenient permit process review and establish affordable permit fees to encourage local and small-scale businesses.

**(5)** Provide easy-to-follow waste disposal, water use and water treatment regulations.

**(6)** Allow commercial uses beyond retail sales, such as workshops, catering kitchens, light industry, commercial services, as well as social services such as childcare, etc.

SHOPPING STREETS

*163*

# WEST BROADWAY

*Missoula, Montana*

As Missoula's Redevelopment Agency considered revitalizing this street, they realized it has the right attributes for expanding commerce:

- It's a highly visible, major arterial "gateway" corridor that also attracts pedestrians and bicyclists.
- The street can be reduced from 4 to 3 lanes and the additional right-of-way repurposed for bikes and pedestrians.
- There are opportunities for temporary and permanent commerce within the right-of-way and on adjoining underutilized roads.

Community workshops and interviews brought residents and businesses into the design process.

# 6

## PLAY ON THE STREET

*Play Streets*

Play is fun and joyful, but it's much more than mere amusement—for centuries thoughtful observers and now scientists have recognized that play is integral to both childhood development and adult life.

Like nutrition and sleep, unstructured play is central to our health, well-being, creativity and intelligence—and to our success as an innovative culture.[1] And with a small amount of programming, creative design and policy changes, the street—especially residential streets—can be a perfect place for everyone to play.

Much of our play is structured and planned, often needs gear or special clothes, a specific place to be, and usually has rules that must be followed. While structured recreation like soccer, baseball, tennis and golf are good for us, they're not considered "play."

Unstructured play is informal, spontaneous, free and imaginative.[2] It's often the result of an unexpected interaction between a person and another person, a thought or the environment. And it can happen in a park, on a corner, in leftover space, in a plaza—and on a street. That interaction brings joy, surprise and fun. For example, in cities most people are concentrating on where they are going and what they have to do, barely acknowledging what they are passing by. But what if you encounter a throne on the street instead of a bench? What if you hear music and see dance steps on the sidewalk? What if you come upon a stationary bicycle that generates electricity for lights as you pedal? Something has interrupted the purely functional urban environment and drawn us into it. The street has sent you a cue that allows you to—for a moment—come out of your role in life and joyfully assume another. That's street play.

**WHY PLAY ON THE STREET?**
Over the years, both time and space for play have declined. While many of us may have played stick ball or tag games on the street, it's unlikely that our children do now. That's of course due to social, cultural and economic trends such as the pressures of education, our busier and sometimes less-active lifestyles, and the perception of safety needs. The increasing popularity of "formal" after-school programs and indoor, technology-based games has actually reduced informal and unstructured play opportunities. And adults have even more limited opportunities for play.

Many countries such as the Netherlands, England, Germany and Australia have very successfully incorporated play into streets. And a great deal of research has demonstrated the importance of incorporating play and leisure amenities into public space, including areas other than parks.[3]

Most modern-day street design has not yet explored the opportunities for play, and the physical environment on the street usually doesn't meet the needs of all users, especially its youngest inhabitants or even adults.

**GOALS**
Unstructured street play can provide opportunities for physical activity, especially in areas that have inadequate parks and open space. A well-designed play street should meet the following goals:

- Bring children and adults outside, connecting people to their neighborhood in a fun and engaging way.
- Allow children and adults to safely socialize with friends and members of their community, ensuring that children are seen as an integral part of community life.
- Improve the health and well-being of all community members, with unstructured play opportunities that are different from play available in parks and playgrounds.

FACING: Dixieanne Avenue, Sacramento. Project design and photo by MIG, Inc.

PLAY STREETS

**169**

• Help everyone learn new skills and explore the environment in which they live.

• Support three major categories of play:

— **Physically active play,** such as basketball, other ball games, skating and stationary bikes that are important for large and fine muscle development, eye-hand-foot coordination, balancing, locomotion, etc. This kind of play also encourages social and cooperative play and helps connect players with the physical environment of the street.

— **Quiet play,** such as reading and chalking, that allows for contemplation, creation and conversation. Like physical play, quiet play also encourages social and cooperative interactions. It provides a balance to physically active play, and can be included in locations where physically active play may not be possible because of space constraints or concerns about noise.

— **Free play,** particularly appropriate to the street setting, that includes dramatic and imaginative play and interesting social interactions.

LEFT: Central Rome. Photo by Catherine Courtenaye/MIG, Inc.

**ACTIVITIES ON A PLAY STREET**

Streets designed for play should provide safe and easily accessible places that contribute to the health and well-being of all members of the community and offer play opportunities that are distinct from play available in parks and playgrounds. Streets for play should allow for a diversity of play activities for people of all ages and abilities.

PLAY · GROW · GREEN · MOVE · GATHER · SHOP ·

PLAY: Exercising, Reading, Building, Discovering, Balancing, Playing games, Climbing, Sensing, Drawing, Geocaching, Jumping, Thinking, Sliding

GROW: Harvesting, Composting, Pruning, Propagating, Weeding, Planting, Mulching, Irrigating, Storing

GREEN: Cleansing water, Distributing materials, Generating energy, Creating habitat, Recycling, Reusing, Managing waste, Harvesting water, Rejuvenating

MOVE: Locating, Parking, Interpreting, Running, Orienting, Biking, Riding, Driving, Walking, Servicing, Strolling, Navigating, Rolling/skating

GATHER: Singing, Meeting, Playing music, Sitting, Talking, Eating, Parading, Learning, Resting, Teaching, Networking, People watching, Demonstrating, Dancing

SHOP: Selling, Bargaining, Performing, Bartering, Displaying, Buying, Browsing, Cooking, Producing, Manufacturing, Dining

## LYMAN PLACE
*New York City*

Lyman Place is a 500 foot-long block in the Bronx that has been closed to traffic every day in the summers from 1980 until 2014. The play street initiative, New York Kids Foundation, was started by Hetty Fox when she moved back to the neighborhood where she had spent her childhood. Growing up there, she says, she learned to ride her bike, played games, danced and learned about conversation, confidence and respect. She wanted to give kids the same opportunity she had had.[4]

It was not easy. Funds were always short. There was no real additional infrastructure, just the barricades to keep cars out, tables, chairs, a basketball hoop, a volleyball net across the street, and the games and crafts the community organized. But the kids—and parents—were out at 8 a.m. sharp every weekday in the summer. The street was a sanctuary for seeing friends and neighbors and just playing. It worked.

Initially, the street was closed from 8 a.m. to 8 p.m. so parents could play with their children when they came home from work. During the last 15 years, police directed that the street closure couldn't extend beyond 5 p.m.

The money situation remained difficult; Fox was dependent on small grants and

LEFT: Lyman Place, New York City. Photo by The Uni Place.

PLAY STREETS

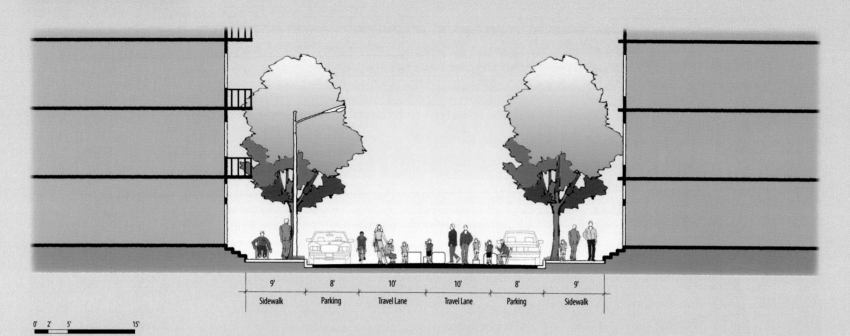

| 9' | 8' | 10' | 10' | 8' | 9' |
|---|---|---|---|---|---|
| Sidewalk | Parking | Travel Lane | Travel Lane | Parking | Sidewalk |

0'  2'  5'          15'

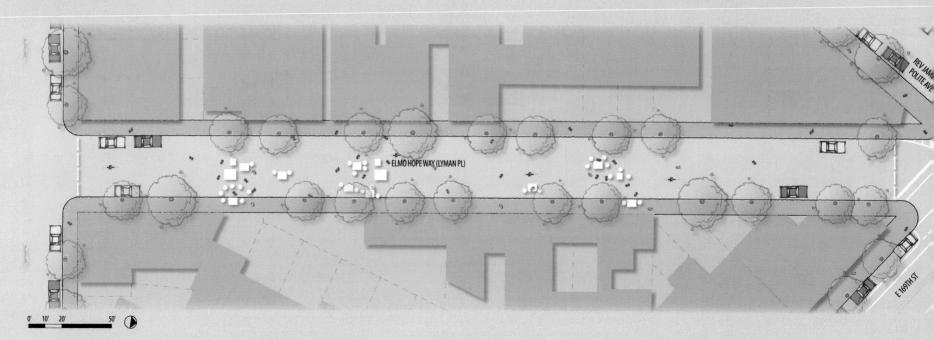

ELMO HOPE WAY (LYMAN PL)

PLAY STREETS

174

REV JAMES POLITE AVE

E 169TH ST

0'  10'  20'        50'

donations to fund supplies. Eventually she had to end the program. However, a second generation of children was able to run and play on the street—a testament to the need for such places in a city's most difficult neighborhoods.

Official play streets in New York City must be on a one-way residential block with no businesses or parking meters. At least 51 percent of residents must sign a petition and the City will provide youth workers to help supervise.

There are other play streets with more benefactors and better equipment; the New York Police Athletic League runs about 75 of them. But Lyman Place was a true, grassroots community effort, much loved by the neighborhood.

RIGHT: Lyman Place, New York City. Photo courtesy Hetty Fox/The Uni Place.

PLAY STREETS

175

**What Works**    It's a one-way street so it can easily be closed off on one end. • Play occurred on the entire street. • The play created both real and perceived safety and community. • The street increased public space for children and families. • Inexpensive programming and equipment was all that was needed. • It created shared memories for several generations.

**Lessons Learned**    Leverage partnerships with other community organizations. • Pursue grants to increase and update programming and equipment. • Get police support for the project. • Plan succession—the street was based on one wonderful person who couldn't be expected to maintain it forever.

# BEECH CROFT ROAD
*Oxford, England*

Residents of this street in the north of Oxford were fed up with a street dominated by cars, especially those cutting through between two busy streets. With the help of Sustrans, a sustainable transport nonprofit dedicated to low-cost street solutions, they got their street back. Beech Croft was Oxford's first Sustrans DIY Street, projects designed to redesign streets and re-focus them on people.

Residents of this street took an unusual route to changing their street. First, they created a living room on the street, with a piano on one side, and comfy sofa, tables and fake TV on the other. "Bumps and chicanes slow cars down a little, but they don't change a driver's psychological state," says Ted Dewan, a resident and activist. Cars driving through a living room really slowed down![5]

Once Sustrans got involved, residents got £8,000, which they combined with a lot of volunteer labor. The entire community helped design the street, laying out stripes of colors and hay bales to indicate where large potted plants might go. The fire department

RIGHT: Beech Croft Road, Oxford. Photo by Jonathan Bewley/Sustrans.

PLAY STREETS

177

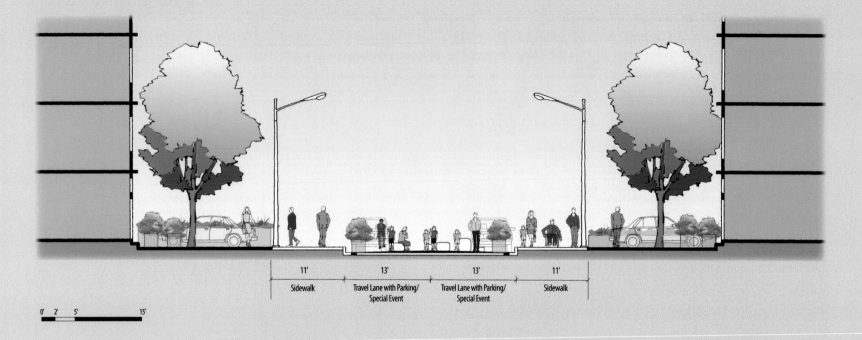

| 11' | 13' | 13' | 11' |
|---|---|---|---|
| Sidewalk | Travel Lane with Parking/ Special Event | Travel Lane with Parking/ Special Event | Sidewalk |

0'   2'   5'                    15'

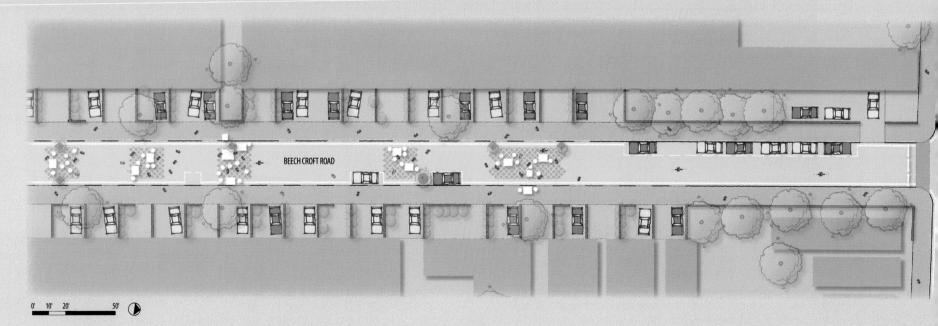

BEECH CROFT ROAD

0'   10'   20'         50'

then drove the street to ensure they'd be able to move their vehicles along the street.

A painted "welcome mat" and a carpet of diamonds virtually yell out "this is a residential area." Residents were a little nonplussed when a huge vat-like planter arrived; no one really wanted it in front of their house. But two young girls soon realized it would look good with a cat face; residents painted a glow-in-the dark "Cheshire cat" that's only seen at night. That planter is now a star of the street.

The road is now an extension of the residents' front gardens. The residents "de-homogenized" the previously straight street, creating obstacles and ambiguous spaces so drivers have to slow down enough to figure out what to do. Meanwhile, children and adults cheerfully play and ride bikes all over the street.

The revamped street opened in October 2010. According to Road Safety Engineering, Oxfordshire County Council, vehicles now drive at about 15 mph, comparable to what speed bumps would accomplish. But a lot friendlier looking.

"When cities are set up in such a way that the experience of being a bus rider, pedestrian or bike rider is actually better than being in a car," Dewan says, "then we'll see huge cultural changes."

RIGHT: Beech Croft Road, Oxford. Photo by Ted Dewan. Licensed under Creative Commons 2.0.

PLAY STREETS

179

**What Works**  Community participation in the design led to increased socializing during and after the project and "ownership" of the street. • Setting out hay bales for emergency access trial runs helps to get city buy-in. • The street is always open to traffic, but it is slower and there is less of it. • Children and adults can play in the street. • Sidewalks are open with no blockages.

**Lessons Learned**  Reduce development time; the long process led to some frustration for community members.

📧 Communities worldwide have found innovative solutions to increasing space for children and adults to play on the street. Each case study provides lessons learned, on which to build the best practices included at the end of this chapter. More information is available at www.reStreets.org.

**MUSIC LIGHTS THE NIGHT** *New Orleans, Louisiana*

In the hard-hit Lower Ninth ward of New Orleans, recovery from Hurricane Katrina was lagging. Only 37 percent of residents had returned as of 2015 and the area was floundering due to a lack of services. Urban Conga[6] decided to create a musical play space and talked with residents about what they would like. Blue cylinders are now grouped to suggest chairs around a table, inviting people to sit, play music and talk. Each cylinder makes a different sound—mostly drumbeats with a few piano tones thrown in. And the cylinders provide light! The roadway has no street lamps and kids were waiting for the bus in the dark many mornings. Now they can drum and light up their mornings. (Nearby businesses provide the electricity, although solar panels may come.)

**PEARL STREET PEDESTRIAN MALL** *Boulder, Colorado*

Pearl Street, the "crown jewel of Boulder," is filled with children and families—and now totally closed to cars.[7] This four-block mall is a child-friendly environment that signals to kids that it is a place to play and be animated. Each block of the mall has a major child-oriented amenity including play boulders, whimsical statues, a pop-jet fountain, a weeping rock and a giant boulder. The community rejected slides and swings, wanting instead to create a more urban experience. The mall also offers shops, restaurants, an information center, landscaping, public restrooms, grassy areas and shady places to sit and relax. As it turns out, play for both adults and children rescued the mall from decline.

### PARK AND SLIDE  *Bristol, England*

Street play isn't just for kids. Bristol, England created a one-day, 300-foot water slide down Park Street in the City center.[8] It was a huge hit. Although only about 350 people would be able to slide, almost 100,000 people signed up! Sliders ranged from 5 years old to 73 years old. The slide incline was 6.5 degrees and people traveled at 11.2 miles per hour on a bed of foam. The creator, Luke Jerram, said the "massive urban slide transforms the street and asks people to take a fresh look at their city...imagine if there were permanent slides right across the City?" The project was totally funded by the community and there's a kit available to help cities create their own slide (small administration fee); contact artwork@lukejerram.com.

### PLAY ME, I'M YOURS  *Sydney, Australia*

Imagine walking down a street and finding a piano sitting right there, for anyone to play. That's what happened in Sydney, Australia and in 45 other cities around the world.[9] The program, started in 2008 and still going strong, works by first soliciting donations of private pianos, then setting them up for at least a 10-day period on the street. In Perth, they were decorated by young people from Western Australia and donated to local schools afterwards. People of all ages and all abilities sat down to play a little tune or two, connecting with their surroundings—and surrounding people who were drawn to the music. Visit streetpianos.com for more information.

### ROSE F. KENNEDY GREENWAY  *Boston, Massachusetts*

The Rose F. Kennedy Greenway is a 1.5-mile, 15-acre linear park that winds through the heart of Boston. It replaced Boston's Central Artery, an elevated highway that ran through Downtown and disconnected communities from one another and the waterfront.[10] Vehicular traffic now runs in a tunnel below the Greenway, leaving open space on top for children and adults to play, and re-connecting some of Boston's oldest neighborhoods. Each segment of the Greenway offers different design features and amenities such as water elements, horticultural displays, demonstration gardens, a carousel, a giant mural, interactive art, farmers markets, labyrinths and options for sitting and relaxing.

Chalk and paint, signage, trees and vegetation, and special pavers make streets feel safe for spontaneous play. Adding elements like climbing walls, play equipment, natural materials and loose parts, interpretive art and temporary lane closures will draw people of all ages to come out and play.

## Art

Art, and opportunities for creating art, provide opportunities for play and learning.

## Climbing walls

Nets or other structures to climb, attached to adjacent buildings, walls and fences, attract people, young and old.

## Lighting

For nighttime visibility and a sense of security, lighting can be designed to enhance the mood or character of a place for play.

## Manufactured play equipment

Permanent or temporary equipment like basketball hoops and table tennis create opportunities for interactions between strangers.

## Natural materials and loose parts

Boulders, rocks, leaves, sand, blocks, etc., provide loose parts for children and adults to manipulate.

## Overhead elements

These can create a "tunnel" or "secret" passageway to encourage fantasy play.

## Sidewalk graphics

Crosswalks painted like piano keys and street games painted on sidewalks or travel lanes encourage social interaction and spontaneous play.

## Signage

Identify places where play is a priority, mark a play street, and provide information, interpretation and directions (such as instructions about games or trails or safety information).

## Specialty lighting

Lighting can provide game patterns or images on the street or building walls.

## Storage areas

Provide lockable cabinets to store loose play equipment, trikes, brooms, etc.

## Drinking water

For people and pets, drinking water can be provided through fountains, water bottle filling stations, etc.

## Exercise equipment

Stationary bikes and exercise steps provide opportunities for large muscle activity and can also serve as a backdrop for social and dramatic play.

## Fun furnishings

Unexpected seating elements like sculptures of animals, game tables and small or oversize chairs encourage lingering.

## Interactive structures

Climbable sculptures and structures with movable gears, steering wheels, funny mirrors, and games stimulate play.

## Paving

A variety of paving types can differentiate play areas from roadway paving, incorporate street games, provide safety surfacing and help with street calming.

## Public restrooms

On commercial streets, this basic amenity can encourage people to gather and stay on the street for extended periods of time.

## Seating

Provide mixed and movable seating, made of materials that are durable and require minimal maintenance.

## Shade-providing elements

Shelters, canopies, arbors, trees, tents, etc., protect people from the elements.

## Temporary traffic blocks

Retractable bollards and movable planter boxes can close ends of streets and calm traffic.

## Trees and vegetation

Trees provide protection from the elements and access to natural materials for play, while also providing habitat for birds, butterflies, etc.

## Trash and recycling receptacles

Provide bins to encourage people to look after public spaces.

## Water access

Provide water for art, sand play, water spray play, gardening and cleanup, etc.

# CREATING A PLAY STREET

Settings for play should be based on the context of the street and truly integrated into the street fabric and not just mimic existing playground environments. Play elements should be visually and physically accessible so people can see what's happening and spontaneously join the fun.

Play is most easily accommodated on streets where traffic speed is reduced and traffic flow is low. Residual spaces on existing streets and on sidewalks can be re-claimed to include play activities. Creating contiguous "play zones," a repetition of play experiences, and locating play in unconventional and surprising locations contribute to a playful street image. Permanent street closures allow for all types of play on the street, while temporary closures allow play on a periodic basis. The streets adjacent to formal play and recreation facilities (parks, playgrounds and schools) are also conducive to providing expanded play opportunities.

Play streets need to work for people of all abilities, following Americans with Disabilities (ADA) guidelines. Some play activities are more appropriate to specific types of streets and specific areas of the street—these best practices will help bring play to *your* streets.

# Keep play safe

**1** Locate play on safe, very low-speed, local, low-volume streets with primarily destination traffic, such as one- or two-block streets and cul-de-sacs.

**2** Locate play on streets with minimal driveways and curb cuts where conflicts with private access is minimal or nonexisting. Address impacts of losing on-street parking during the time of street play.

**3** Incorporate traffic-calming elements on streets not closed to traffic to ensure traffic speed is 5 mph on local residential "play streets" and 15 mph on local mixed-use streets—where play is allowed only on sidewalks.

**4** Install permanent speed tables (much wider than speed humps) to demarcate a special area and slow cars down. These allow road surfaces to be at grade with the sidewalk, thereby enhancing the pedestrian experience.

**5** Use different design interventions such as temporary or permanent bulb outs, to narrow the two ends of a play section, either at both ends of a street or mid-street if only a section of the street will be for play.

**6** Create temporary daytime or seasonal street closures by using retractable bollards, movable planter boxes or straw bales to allow for play beyond the sidewalk, even on heavily trafficked local streets. Large pots and planter boxes can be moved to streets that serve as temporary play streets.

**7** Incorporate greenery such as trees and plantings in bulb outs or above surface in large pots and planter boxes that serve to narrow the road and decrease speed as cars negotiate tighter spaces (while still allowing for emergency vehicles). This can be especially helpful at intersections.

**8** Apply play area safety standards as required, including synthetic safety surfacing under climbing elements, for example.

**9** Locate play areas that are visible from residences, shops or other nearby areas.

PLAY STREETS

*187*

## Intervene at different scales as appropriate

**1** Create small and medium-size play points at bulb outs, bus stops, stoops, walls and fences, intersections and even parking spaces that are permanently or temporarily closed.

**2** Create play pathways that flow from the linear pattern of the street, along sidewalks, parking lanes, medians and temporarily closed travel lanes.

**3** Create play streets using the entire length and width of a street on streets permanently or temporarily closed to traffic, on wide sidewalk streets and in alleys.

**4** Repurpose underutilized parking lanes and individual parking spaces to allow play on local residential, commercial and mixed-use streets.

## Make play affordable to build and maintain

**1** Ensure that play elements are sturdy, built to withstand public use and easily repaired or replaced.

**2** Repurpose lights and utility poles as poles for hanging basketball hoops and volleyball nets.

**3** Design stormwater planters to provide opportunities for free play.

**4** Repurpose seating slabs for jumping games, chess tables, etc.

**5** Allow adjacent storage areas on private properties for loose parts and tools for self-cleanup, such as brooms, etc.

**6** Provide low-cost loose part play kits to groups organizing play streets.

**7** Enact policies that make it easier to close streets temporarily and to streamline more permanent changes to the street such as installing bulb outs and special paving.

**8** Enact policies to provide funding to community groups for maintenance and special play events.

# Encourage active play

**1** Provide infrastructure for active games, such as hoops for basketball, goals for soccer, ball walls, sleeves for nets of ball games such as volleyball, etc.

**2** Use paving patterns to encourage pavement games.

**3** Provide outdoor exercise equipment such as stationary bikes, climbing walls, exercise steps, parallel bars, etc.

**4** Locate seating areas near play elements. Provide a variety of seating that is comfortable and convenient, like "plop benches" that are larger in size than regular benches and provide caregivers extra space to sit with all of their belongings while children play.

**5** Create mobile play units that can travel and bring play to the street in a variety of neighborhoods.

**6** Include design elements such as drums, musical instruments, ping-pong and large scrabble sets that appeal to both children and adults and encourage them to play together.

**7** Incorporate elements that accommodate sports, such as skating lanes or skateboard runs and street surfacing that is suitable for running and jogging.

## Encourage quiet play

**1** Include drawing stations with easels, seating and access to water.

**2** Provide reading and storytelling nooks and lending libraries with comfortable seating, protected from the sun, wind and rain.

**3** Provide surfaces for drawing and stenciling on the street surface or walls.

**4** Include interpretive signage, murals, artifacts, etc., to describe the historical or ecological context of place or stories about the neighborhood.

**5** Include loose parts and natural materials, such as sand, water, small rocks and twigs that encourage creative play.

**6** Provide child-sized street furnishings adjacent to adult furnishings so families can play together.

**7** Include sculptures that are based on the local flora and fauna.

# Encourage free play

**1** Provide cues that encourage the public to interact with interpretive signage, art elements, discovery maps and audio.

**2** Provide natural play elements like boulders and trees for climbing.

**3** Set up stage-like areas to prompt imaginative and dramatic play.

**4** Use plants that attract insects such as butterflies.

**5** Design paving patterns to encourage pavement games.

**6** Include windmills, wind chimes, or solar-powered items that respond to natural elements.

**7** Include play features that invite exploration and discovery.

## Provide a "human infrastructure"

**1** Form community partnerships to take ownership of play elements and programs.

**2** Involve community members, especially children and youth, in design, construction and maintenance.

**3** Promote upcoming programs and special events.

**4** Organize seasonal neighborhood events such as "summer camps" that include play activities on the street.

**5** Organize play events that use loose parts and allow for play on a temporary basis.

**6** Employ trained neighborhood play leaders as "ambassadors" to champion play and organize events on the street.

**7** Encourage play activities that are low-cost and require little or no effort, such as chalk.

**8** Use social media to connect parents and children to play opportunities in the neighborhood and on the street.

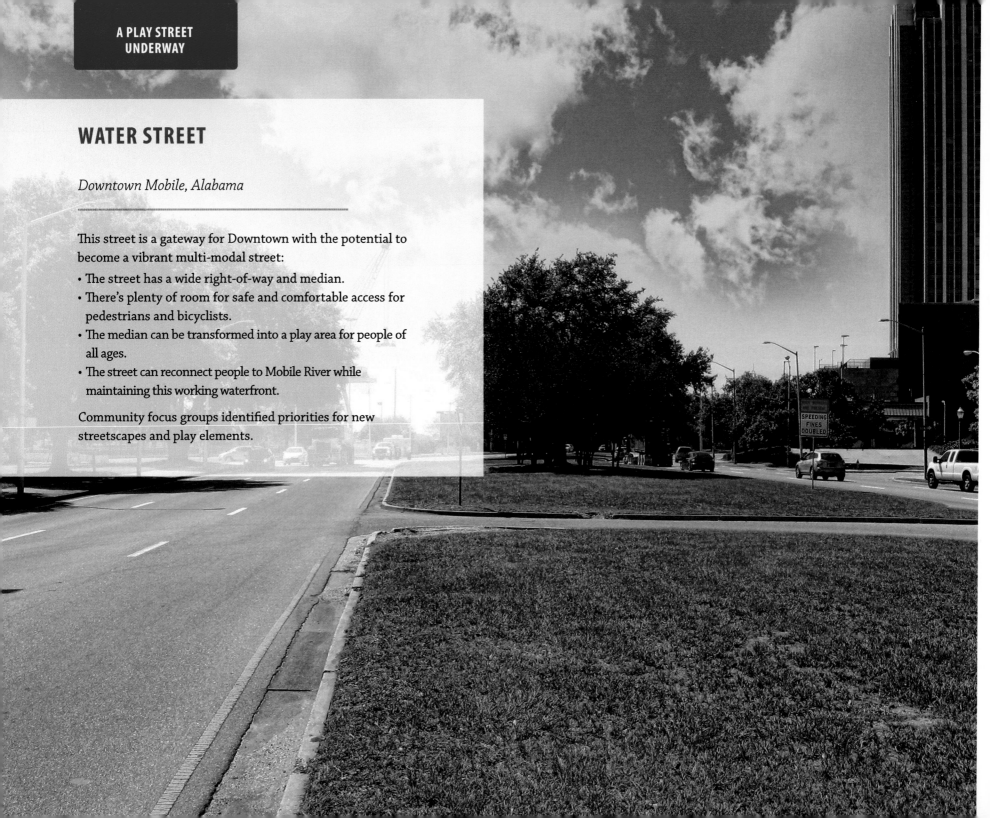

# WATER STREET

*Downtown Mobile, Alabama*

This street is a gateway for Downtown with the potential to become a vibrant multi-modal street:

• The street has a wide right-of-way and median.
• There's plenty of room for safe and comfortable access for pedestrians and bicyclists.
• The median can be transformed into a play area for people of all ages.
• The street can reconnect people to Mobile River while maintaining this working waterfront.

Community focus groups identified priorities for new streetscapes and play elements.

# 7

## GROW ON THE STREET

*Farm Streets*

At the intersection of the public realm, the "eat local" movement, and the lack of local fresh food in many urban neighborhoods,[1] lies urban agriculture: food grown on the street for the local community. How we choose to produce and distribute food has far-reaching effects on the community fabric, health, regional and local development, ecological security, economic development and social justice. Urban agriculture in the public right-of-way can become a vital, nourishing and energizing element of the street scene—especially on neighborhood streets.

Food is not just a simple set of substances that nourish our bodies. The worldwide food revolution has many people more closely examining what we put in our mouths, where it comes from, the quality of ingredients, additives, and energy costs to grow and transport it.

By 2050, global population will increase by as many as 3 billion people—even by the most conservative estimates—and nearly 80 percent will reside in urban centers. Our highly industrialized society, with easy access to fuel for food production and transportation, has made agriculture an almost exclusively rural activity.[2] This wasn't always the case—we have a long history of growing food near where we live, a practice we renew in times of need. For example, during World War II, "Victory Gardens" in the United States provided food to urban residents. If we follow traditional farming practices, we'll need an estimated 1 billion hectares of new land (about 20 percent more land than in Brazil) to grow enough food to feed them.[3, 4, 5] The consequence of deforesting all that new land for agriculture could be devastating to the environment.

**WHY FARM ON THE STREET?**
With the movement to free up land for non-auto related use within existing rights-of-way, streets present a great opportunity for growing food. That's even more beneficial in built-out urban areas with poor access to fresh, affordable produce.

Streets allow both horizontal and vertical spaces to be used for plants. Horizontally, plants are in the ground or in raised beds in areas that might ordinarily be devoted to landscaping, such as planting strips, medians, and bulb outs, or in reclaimed paved areas like parking lanes. Plants can also be grown on rooftops. Vertically, plants can be grown in areas not usually used for vegetation, such as attached to walls and fences, hung from supports, and trained on arbors along or over a sidewalk.

The simple act of growing a street tomato for local consumption can build local community, improve nutrition intake and overall health, reduce productivity burdens on far-off farms, reduce transportation costs and impacts, reduce pesticide and fertilizer applications and impacts, nurture the local ecosystem, educate the community in biology and nutrition and reduce food costs. It may seem a lot to ask of one tomato, but if the full impact of street agriculture is drawn out, it can make a significant contribution to global food supply.

The current applications of urban agriculture are varied and diverse—from community gardens to high-tech vertical gardens, and from cities with highly coordinated and organized agriculture systems and policies to local, grass-roots organizations with little or no governmental support.

Many cities and towns are already addressing the level of support required (in terms of regulation and funding) and the design requirements necessary to make urban agriculture work throughout their urban areas. Some are formally incorporating agriculture in the street rights-of-way by developing policies that support the participation of community residents. While programs must be customized to the local context, this chapter offers a replicable methodology for accommodating and establishing street agriculture on the street.

FARM STREETS

199

## GOALS

Urban agriculture on the street should aim to meet four overall goals:

**Improve general health and well-being**
- Increase access to reasonably priced or free healthy food
- Reconnect urban dwellers with the food system
- Provide education about nutrition

**Strengthen communities**
- Enhance community connections
- Increase a sense of community ownership

**Better use of the public realm**
- Increase the functional use of the public realm and thereby return greater value to taxpayers

- Increase vegetation and green spaces in urban neighborhoods
- Strengthen the urban habitat and support a diversity of insects and animals

**Provide opportunities for entrepreneurship**
- Build new skill sets in the community
- Potentially create jobs

**GROW**
- Propagating
- Pruning
- Composting
- Weeding
- Planting
- Harvesting
- Mulching
- Storing
- Irrigating

**GREEN**
- Distributing materials
- Cleansing water
- Generating energy
- Creating habitat
- Recycling
- Reusing
- Managing waste
- Harvesting water
- Rejuvenating

**MOVE**
- Parking
- Interpreting
- Running
- Orienting
- Biking
- Riding
- Driving
- Locating
- Walking
- Rolling/skating
- Navigating
- Strolling
- Servicing

**GATHER**
- Singing
- Dancing
- Meeting
- Demonstrating
- Playing music
- People watching
- Sitting
- Networking
- Talking
- Eating
- Teaching
- Parading
- Learning
- Resting

**SHOP**
- Selling
- Bargaining
- Performing
- Bartering
- Displaying
- Buying
- Browsing
- Cooking
- Producing
- Manufacturing
- Dining

**PLAY**
- Sensing
- Climbing
- Playing games
- Balancing
- Discovering
- Building
- Reading
- Exercising
- Drawing
- Geocaching
- Jumping
- Thinking
- Sliding

**ACTIVITIES ON A FARM STREET**
Medians, sidewalk planters and underused bits of space can be repurposed for growing food—both vertically and horizontally. Depending on the amount of space available, urban agricultural activities can be chosen and combined to maximize food production and community building.

# WILGA AVENUE VERGE GARDENS

*Sydney, Australia*

Wilga Avenue is just a block long, but that short block is packed with verge gardens— little gardens between the sidewalk and the curb. It all began in 2009 when a few moms were out with their children. The street and 10 foot-wide sidewalks were an almost continuous sheet of pavement, and the heat radiating off them was intense during the hot Sydney summers. The neighbors realized that if they removed some of the concrete between the curb and the sidewalk path of travel and replaced it with planted gardens, they could bring some life to the street and cool it at the same time.

A few families got together and started breaking down the "bitumenscape" on the weekends, planting veggies, fruits and native plants. Gradually, more neighbors got involved. One verge garden now holds a little picnic table under an arbor where people gather and children eat snacks. The community often has gatherings out on the street, which is a cul-de-sac. Residents say that gardening has brought life out from backyards and playrooms onto the street, and that they truly value feeling that they are part of a strong, caring neighborhood.

LEFT: Wilga Avenue. Photo by Leonie McNamara.

RIGHT: Wilga Avenue. Photo by Leonie McNamara.

⟩ FARM STREETS

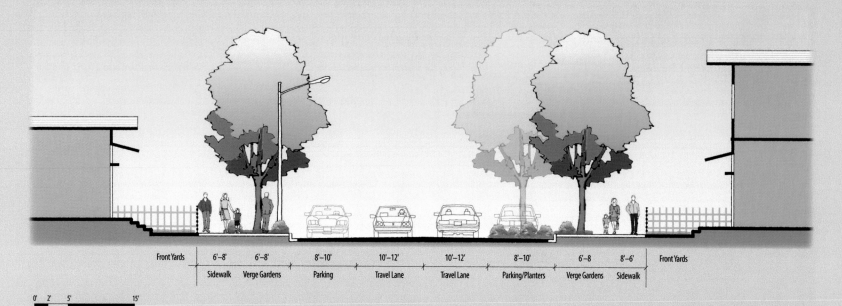

Front Yards | 6'–8' | 6'–8' | 8'–10' | 10'–12' | 10'–12' | 8'–10' | 6'–8 | 8'–6' | Front Yards

Sidewalk | Verge Gardens | Parking | Travel Lane | Travel Lane | Parking/Planters | Verge Gardens | Sidewalk

0'    2'    5'                    15'

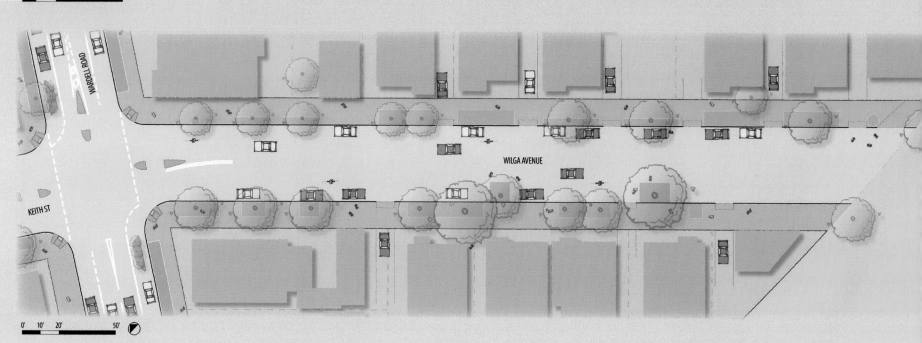

WARDELL ROAD

WILGA AVENUE

KEITH ST

0'    10'    20'                    50'

The verge gardens occupy approximately six feet of the sidewalk, with four feet as a clear path of travel. Residents installed rainwater-harvesting pipes under sidewalks, which bring water from their rooftops to the gardens. The neighborhood also has a worm bin and five chickens. Neighbors share veggies and eggs, and say that the closeness of the neighborhood leads them to share much more. All eleven houses on the block have planted verges, and each maintains its own.

In 2011, the neighborhood was named the most sustainable street in Sydney by Origin Energy, an Australian utility company. Residents received free sustainable power for a year and solar panels for their homes. The verge gardens were established without City involvement, but were so popular that they inspired Sydney to develop a strong urban gardening program, including verge gardening design guidelines.

**FARM STREETS**

207

**What Works** It's convenient to grow and harvest food. • Neighbors come together through shared effort and natural socializing. • Children learn about gardening and ecological systems. • Carbon emissions are reduced with zero food miles travelled. • The urban heat island effect is mitigated and the street is more appealing. • Impermeable surfaces and stormwater runoff are reduced.

**Lessons Learned** Planting food in areas accessible to people and cars can be challenging because soil may be contaminated, plants and crops may be taken or trampled, and pets may soil the area. • Low-traffic areas may be better suited to food crops. • Maintenance may be an issue, especially with food crops and inexperienced gardeners. • Drivers need easy access to parked cars.

# GILMAN GARDENS

*Seattle, Washington*

What was an overgrown, trash-strewn hillside and haphazard parking area is now a lush community garden that has beautified the street and brought the community together. Plus, it produces tasty food!

Gilman Gardens is located on a residual space separating the busy north- and southbound lanes of Gilman Drive West. It's an irregular, 40-foot wide and 230-foot-long median.

All cities have overlooked little spots such as where there are gaps in grade, triangles where streets meet at odd angles, unused medians and extra wide pedestrian travel paths. Seattle is a trailblazer in encouraging gardens, with its 40-year-old P-Patch Program that now offers an online process for garden permits, grants, tools and other resources. Each year Seattle gardens grow and donate more than 10 tons of produce to neighborhood food banks.

Much of the beauty of Gilman Gardens comes from the way that it has been shaped by each gardener. The 20-plot garden is planted and maintained by community members. Raised beds are

FARM STREETS

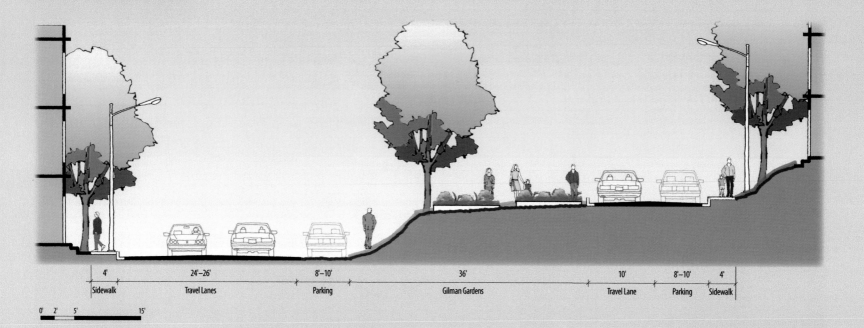

| 4' | 24'–26' | 8'–10' | 36' | 10' | 8'–10' | 4' |
|---|---|---|---|---|---|---|
| Sidewalk | Travel Lanes | Parking | Gilman Gardens | Travel Lane | Parking | Sidewalk |

0'  2'  5'          15'

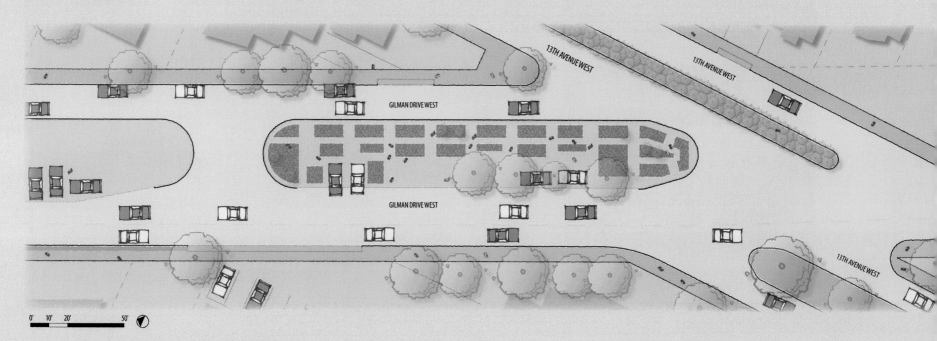

13TH AVENUE WEST

13TH AVENUE WEST

GILMAN DRIVE WEST

GILMAN DRIVE WEST

13TH AVENUE WEST

0'  10'  20'          50'

supported by a variety of materials, including wooden planks, woven sticks and cement locks. Because the garden is located on a hillside, each plot is a terrace. One side may be at ground level while the other serves as a bench.

A small central shed provides storage space for tools and a seed exchange. A basket set atop an orange stool serves as an informal vegetable exchange. There is a central community area and they've even conducted a wedding there! The garden is unfenced and open to the public.

In the first year, gardeners watered their plots by bringing buckets of water from home or filling them at nearby properties. Some rainwater harvesting systems were then put in place. The gardeners plan to raise enough money to install a water connection, but much of the water used for irrigation is still gathered in orange rain barrels scattered through the garden.

Demand for gardening space is high, so an adjacent median now has another 20 plots.

RIGHT: Gilman Gardens, Seattle. Photo by by MIG, Inc.

FARM STREETS

**211**

**What Works**  Food is grown on residual spaces • An unsightly median attracted illegal behavior and dumping and has now been reclaimed for public use. • The garden supports local community ties and individual expression • Experience growing food and plants ties the community more closely to ecological systems. • The garden design adapts to locally available materials and land forms.

**Lessons Learned**  Watering the garden without a water connection is difficult and a limiting factor. • Garden administration and maintenance are challenging when it's all volunteer.

 Communities worldwide have found innovative solutions to finding space for agriculture on the street. These case studies provide lessons learned, on which to build the best practices included at the end of this chapter. More information about these projects and programs is available on www.reStreets.org.

### DESERT HARVESTERS  *Tucson, Arizona*

We don't usually think of harvests in an urban desert, but what began as a roadside experiment is turning Tucson into a food garden. In 1996, Brad Lancaster watched as precious summer monsoon rain sheeted down the drain. He cut a length of curb in front of his house and allowed rainwater to collect at the base of a Mesquite tree. Neighbors saw and replicated it. The City of Tucson got involved and formalized a rain garden program, with bulb outs and traffic circles, maintained by neighbors. In Lancaster's neighborhood, they planted more than 1,200 Mesquite, Desert Ironwood, and Screwbean trees, which produce edible beans and pods— and shade the street. Residents even earn money using the ground mesquite flour in baked goods sold at farmers markets and at the annual Mesquite Pancake Breakfast.[6]

### JUST GET RID OF THE PAVEMENT  *Gurgaon, India*

Once a small agricultural village, Gurgaon is now a hub of multinational companies and skyscrapers about 20 miles west of New Delhi. Its densely built Sector 14 Main Road featured 15-foot-wide paved rights-of-way along the street that had been privatized for parking. That was just too much concrete for some residents. They simply dug up a 10-foot section and planted it with potatoes, spinach, eggplants, onions, turnips, parsnips, radishes and herbs. There's still a 4-foot raised sidewalk next to the travel lane for pedestrians, but now many families share the food and enjoy the lack of pavement. The road is also a route for children walking to school, who are allowed to "steal" one item to munch on each way, as they say hello to the "auntiji" and "uncleji," owners of the edible garden patch.[7]

**QUESADA AVENUE** *San Francisco, California*

The Hunters View/Baypoint Quesada neighborhood was an unsafe place to live because of drug dealers, crime and trash dumping, with many vacant houses and abandoned vehicles—and it lacked grocery stores and parks. In 2002, the community decided to take its street back. With about 30 residents as co-founders, they began with the Quesada Avenue median strip, about 600 feet long and 20 feet wide, with a designated traffic speed of 15 mph. After that success, neighbors developed 20 backyard gardens, nine community gathering spaces, two major murals, public art projects, and a stream of popular community events. The median remains the hub of a shared food program in the neighborhood, centered on families, churches and long-standing affinity group social networks.[8, 9]

**PASONA VERTICAL GARDEN** *Tokyo, Japan*

Pasona HQ is a visual intervention into busy urban lifestyles, designed to promote direct farm-to-table projects in Tokyo. The building exterior was dramatically renovated with a living façade, growing oranges and flowers in 3-foot-deep balconies that are wrapped with a deep grid of fins to create further depth and volume for the plants. The plants create a green wall that shades and insulates the building, increasing energy efficiency. Inside the nine-story building is 40,000 square feet of agriculture, featuring 200 species of fruits, vegetables and rice, with tomato vines growing over conference tables, a broccoli field in reception, lemon and passion fruit trees as partitions, salad leaves sprouting in seminar rooms and bean sprouts growing under benches. The building now provides enough food for all employees.[10, 11]

**FRUIT TREE STREETS** *Davis, California*

The 1964 Village Homes development was designed to increase a sense of community while conserving energy and natural resources.[12] It incorporates edible landscapes on street medians and planter areas, in addition to an orchard. Residents can pick oranges, apricots, nectarines, peaches, pears, persimmons, almonds, cherries and plums. The trees grow to be about 10 to 15 feet high and 10 feet wide, and they're planted about 8 feet from the curb so their limbs don't hang over the street. The wide variety of fruit guarantees that there's always something ripe to pick and annual harvest festivals bring the community together. Residents now produce about 25 percent of their household fruits and nuts on the street.[13]

The critical elements to create a garden are planting beds and a water source. Adding ready access to garden amenities, storage, compost bins and seating and other elements provides a richer experience and more compelling reasons for people to grow and share food.

### Art

Interpretive and engaging art can be based on agriculture, created on-site, and provide opportunities for learning.

### Cold storage boxes

Containers can be swap boxes for fruits and vegetables, keeping them stored at cool temperatures.

### Gardening shed

Bins or other structures can store tools and other supporting equipment and double as a potting shed.

### Ground planting beds

Ground-level beds work well in small areas, but should be well away from the flow of urban stormwater.

### Lighting

Lighting is important for nighttime visibility and a sense of security.

### Paving

A variety of paving types can differentiate areas from roadway paving, indicate where food is being grown and help with street calming.

### Signage

Visually identify places where food is being grown, "do's and don'ts" and provide safety information, interpretation and directions.

### Structures

Arbors, pergolas, and tents can provide shade, support vertical planting and function as gathering spots.

### Temporary traffic blocks

Movable planter boxes and containers can be used to grow food and block traffic if the street is to be closed at times (or used as decoration along sidewalks and restaurants).

### Trash and recycling receptacles

Receptacles are essential for maintaining cleanliness and an attractive public space.

### Compost bins

Composting is a handy way to recycle green waste such as leaves and food bits, to be used as a fertilizer and soil amendment.

### Fencing

Whether it demarks private property or is in the public realm, fencing provides structural support for growing food vertically.

### Furniture

Fixed and movable tables and seating, including raised bed walls, made of durable materials that require minimal maintenance provide comfortable surfaces.

### Garden amenities

Consider including items like a barbecue, greenhouse, cold frame and root shed.

### Power source

Electricity or onsite solar panels or windmills can power mechanized irrigation systems, additional lights, and equipment.

### Protective nets

Various shapes and sizes of netting can protect food from hungry birds and pet waste.

### Public restrooms

On commercial streets, this basic amenity can encourage people to gather and stay for extended periods of time.

### Raised planting beds

Raised beds work well in sidewalk planting areas and medians, allow more efficient use of water, with built-in drainage, keep soil in place and eliminate erosion.

### Trees and vegetation

Trees provide shade for people and habitat for birds, as well as fruits and nuts to eat.

### Vertical planting structures

Walls, trellises and vertically stacked cells provide opportunities for planting where space and access to sunlight are limited—hydroponic systems may require more intensive irrigation.

### Water source

Depending on climate and growing method, plants could be rain-fed, hand-watered using a nearby spigot, or watered via an irrigation system.

# CREATING A FARM STREET

Street agriculture can be implemented in many ways, based on community needs and constraints including community interest, the amount of land available and access to sunlight and water. The U.S. National Garden Bureau states that an entire family of four can be fed from only 600 square feet of land.[14] This can be achieved on a farm street. For example, a street with a 100-foot right-of-way might have a 40-foot planted median, 7- to 8-foot sidewalk planter, 5- to 6-foot pedestrian travel path, and a traffic lane in each direction. On this street, a house with just a 40-foot frontage would have 640 square feet of sidewalk and shared median space on which to grow food.

Depending on what and how food is grown, return on investment can be anywhere from 10 to 25 times costs, and a well-maintained food garden can yield about ½ pound of fresh produce per square foot of garden area.[15] The specific benefits such as improved access to healthy food and social equity will depend on the scale and type of planted area. There are many resources to help start gardens themselves; these best practices will help bring them to *your* streets.

FARM STREETS

## Locate gardens for productivity and safety

① Locate gardens in communities that have expressed interest in community gardens and a willingness to maintain them.

② Provide urban agriculture in high-density neighborhoods where access to private open space is scarce.

③ Locate agriculture on streets with maximum traffic speeds of 20 mph, so gardening activities can be conducted safely and conveniently.

④ Target residential streets with a right-of-way of 50 feet or more and relatively low traffic volumes.

⑤ Ensure that planting beds do not impede on a contiguous ADA-compliant pedestrian path.

⑥ Locate gardens in planting strips on either side of the sidewalk, in medians, roundabouts, bulb outs, planters, interstitial spaces or vertical installations.

⑦ Provide a minimum of a 2-foot buffer for planted areas from the adjoining parking lane to allow car doors to open and for passengers to enter and exit a car.

⑧ If the planted area is in a median or sidewalk next to a travel lane, provide approximately 3 feet as a buffer from the face of the curb.

⑨ Leave room for loading areas for moving equipment and produce, and to accommodate farmers markets, picnics and cooking demonstrations.

⑩ Provide seating and small multi-purpose structures that serve as storage areas for common tools, seeds, etc.

**Examine all possibilities!**

**1** Consider using local commercial streets for urban agriculture, provided that the needs of adjacent street uses can be accommodated.

**2** Consider using underutilized or striped areas between two streets that intersect at odd angles, if safe and convenient pedestrian and vehicular access are available.

**3** Locate vertical gardens in areas where little ground space is available. Community-managed installations may be particularly well suited to long, windowless building walls.

# Design functional planter beds

**1** Ensure that soil holds water and has good drainage. A sandy clay loam soil mixed with compost is best for most plants in raised beds. For shallow-rooted plants such as lettuces and herbs, provide 8–12 inches of soil. To grow a wider range of crops, soil depth should be between 18 and 24 inches.

**2** Ideally, design raised beds as bottomless frames set into a shallow trench.

**3** Align rows to benefit maintenance and irrigation needs.

**4** Generally, allocate 3 feet by 6 feet as a standard planting bed dimension. This is big enough to support plant growth, but small enough to reach easily from both sides.

**5** Design the raised bed to be 1–2 feet tall. Higher beds may require additional soil or a rock base layer.

**6** The sides can be any durable building material with capacity and drainage that is untreated and non-toxic (lumber, layers of rock, cinder blocks, brick, concrete blocks, watering troughs, tubs).

**7** Where possible, use a flat space so that bed walls are level. Align rows to benefit maintenance and irrigation needs.

**8** Provide a minimum of 18 inches between beds for walkways and maintenance and a minimum of 36 inches for wheelchair accessibility and along major pathways.

**9** Ensure a proportionate number of planters are 17–19 inches high to be universally accessible and incorporate a 12-inch wide work surface.

## Appropriately site vertical gardens

**1** Integrate vertical gardens within new building facades.

**2** Locate vertical gardens next to undesirable pedestrian edges such as blank walls and fences of adjoining land uses. Where possible, large, sturdy, continuous, accessible walls can be used to attach plants.

**3** Vertical gardens can be grown along private fences or buildings, with permission of the owner. Users of adjoining buildings should not be impacted by the height of the vertical walls.

**4** Minimize the gap between the vertical garden and walls.

**5** Site vertical gardens for ease of maintenance and operations.

**6** In places with harsh winter conditions, living walls may have a dormancy period and may need extra attention to appear attractive all year.

FARM STREETS

221

## Account for sunlight and wind

**1** In the northern hemisphere, plants should generally be south-facing (and north-facing in the southern hemisphere).

**2** Orient the long axis of the planting area in a north-south direction to maximize sun exposure.

**3** Locate the planting area to minimize the effects of shadows cast by nearby buildings and trees.

**4** Ensure that the planting area receives about 6–8 hours of direct sunlight per day during the growing season.

**5** Grow plants that meet different sunlight and environmental constraints.

**6** In areas prone to high winds, screen plants and use an irrigation system that reduces evaporation.

## Select an appropriate planting palette

**1** Select plants and trees that grow well in the local climate or micro-climate.

**2** Minimize use of plants that grow taller than 36 inches that might provide places to hide and prune fruit trees along sidewalks to ensure ADA access.

**3** Plant sturdier plants and fruit trees along edges to withstand automobile and foot traffic.

**4** In small spaces, avoid crops that take a lot of space, like winter squash.

**5** Avoid high-value products that can be stolen, such as watermelons or sweet corn, unless appropriately fenced and monitored by the community.

**6** Consider a variety of planting plans—from aesthetic, non-edible indigenous plants to fruits and vegetables—as a single crop and in complementary crop patterns and relationships.

FARM STREETS

223

## Manage for pests and toxins

**1** Diversify vegetables to minimize damage from any one pest or disease and monitor planted areas regularly to check for any changes or disease.

**2** Use nets to cover plants and protect them from birds and pets.

**3** Establish plants that provide habitat and food sources for beneficial insects such as ladybugs.

**4** Incorporate natural pest management by introducing insects that feed on pests, like predatory wasps.

**5** Ensure timely harvest management so that food is not left to waste or rot.

**6** To avoid waste matter on edibles, raise planters to a height that is out of reach for larger pets.

**7** Use raised beds to avoid potentially toxic urban runoff and stormwater from streets flowing into beds.

(8) Practice seasonal crop rotation to reduce soil-borne diseases and to help maintain soil structure and fertility.

(9) Create a holistic ecological connection to the larger green infrastructure network to create opportunities for beneficial animal and insect species to use the area.

(10) Select appropriate planting species to minimize and mitigate any toxins present in the soil or when irrigated by rainwater.

(11) Use only non-treated wood and non-toxic materials where food plants are growing.

(12) If using existing on-site soil, conduct soil analysis regularly by a reputable lab, especially at the initial stage.

## Experiment with irrigation systems

(1) Irrigate at appropriate times of the day when the water will have a chance to infiltrate and not simply be evaporated away.

(2) Use a battery-operated, automatic-control timer connected to an exterior faucet or hose-bib attachment. Use in combination with a hose end backflow preventer to prevent any contaminated water from re-entering a domestic water line.

(3) Use a pressure regulator downstream of the timer to reduce incoming water pressure to protect the drip system from having tubing pop off the fittings.

(4) Consider the soil type of the areas to be irrigated when selecting the spacing and flow of the drip emitters.

(5) Use a ½-inch poly tubing mainline as a distribution system, which can be buried underneath mulch.

(6) Water can be distributed using a combination of ¼-inch poly tubing with mini-jet sprayers or point-source emission devices and in-line emitter poly tubing to deliver water directly to plants.

(7) Use a drip filter, with a minimum 120-mesh screen, downstream of the timer to remove sediment and other particles that may clog drip irrigation emitters. Pressure-regulating filters combine both the pressure regulator and filter into one unit.

(8) Consider the water requirements of each plant grouping and develop watering zones based on similar plants watering frequency requirements. It may be possible to maintain a single zone by providing additional emitters or sprayers focused on the plants with higher water requirements.

## Integrate rainwater-harvesting systems

**1** When using rainwater harvesting, carefully select appropriate planting species to minimize and mitigate any toxins present in the rainwater.

**2** Use potable water to irrigate food plants that will be consumed by humans.

**3** Design water storage according to local climatic conditions.

**4** Use companion planting methods to create density and to shade the soil, lowering evapotranspiration.

**5** Integrate bioswales/rain gardens in sidewalk level planting areas and at street level to capture, filter and infiltrate rainwater into the ground.

FARM STREETS

**227**

## Provide supportive human infrastructure

(1) Work with government agency staff to follow local regulations and zoning.

(2) Consider fulfilling part or all on-site open space requirements with community gardens in the street right-of-way, especially in adjoining residual areas.

(3) Explore incentives to reduce on-street parking while providing opportunities for urban agriculture within the street right-of-way.

(4) Where food is grown for selling, especially on residual areas next to the road, modify and change zoning regulations to allow the selling, buying and storage of food.

(5) Create a volunteer organization with a designated volunteer coordinator who interacts with government staff to communicate and address neighborhood issues and needs.

(6) Engage the community in designing gardens and in constructing them, especially in shared planting areas.

(7) Share produce with neighbors using cold storage boxes where possible, and educate passers-by to build goodwill.

(8) Install information kiosks on the street that explain the benefits of urban agriculture, the direct benefits of sustainable food and associated benefits of rain gardens and sustainable infrastructure.

(9) Provide guidelines and training for installing and maintaining urban agriculture through social media, face-to-face workshops and mass media.

**10** Organize community policing and encourage neighbors and neighbor gardeners to keep an eye on the lots to minimize vandalism and crop loss.

**11** Work with both visitors and adjoining residents and business owners not actively engaged in the urban agriculture project to increase awareness and understanding.

**12** Actively engage private sector businesses, churches, and residents in maintaining and harvesting produce.

**13** Engage children and teenagers through volunteerism and paid stipends to encourage working in the garden and harvesting to benefit the needy, while learning about nutrition and healthy living.

**14** Form partnerships with various food venues, including food banks or low-income meal sites, cafes and restaurants.

**15** Coordinate with a network of Master Gardeners to provide training to community members.

**16** Build partnerships with schools, youth organizations and farmers markets.

# FOURTH STREET

*Boyle Heights, Los Angeles, California*

This local residential street, in an area with poor access to affordable, fresh produce, can bring the farm to home:

• There's plenty of foot traffic when residents walk to shops, school and churches.

• The wide 8' planting areas along sidewalks allow residents to grow a wide variety of food.

• The street can also be programmed for buying and selling food.

Based on community meetings, residents didn't want just bike lanes; they wanted to make the street part of their lives.

# 8

## GENERATE ON THE STREET

*Resilient Streets*

Under our feet and over our heads is the maze of pipes and wires that keep our cities functioning—for water, electricity, phones, cable, gas, sewer and material waste. We move through these conveyance systems without much noticing. But, right there, at our feet, are opportunities to transform infrastructure elements into valuable resources.

New and still developing technology can capture and cleanse water; increase groundwater recharge; reduce, recycle and transform waste; increase habitat; and reduce, conserve and even generate energy. The resilient street. This is the future of streets.

**WHY CREATE RESILIENT STREETS?**

Much has been written about the definitions of environmental sustainability and resiliency. On a street, resiliency is the ability of the street ecosystem to be self-sufficient, responding to human activities and natural events by absorbing and mitigating impacts, maintaining desired services and regenerating itself.

Cities and streets are very energy intensive to construct, operate and maintain. Yet during the United Nations Conference on Climate Change it was clear that the real action on combating climate change is taking place locally, in cities, in neighborhoods and on streets, with a micro-level, incremental approach.

Many communities have already developed "green streets" with natural elements like rainwater planters and rain gardens that reduce stormwater flow while naturally cleansing it. Those streets offer aesthetic and visual appeal and provide a glimpse into the usually hidden stormdrain system.

Now let's expand on that. Streets offer a huge piece of public real estate that can be used for much more than passive conveyance and mitigation. Resilient streets provide one of the greatest opportunities for cities to achieve their sustainability goals, increase available water and habitat, reduce greenhouse gas emissions, transform waste and generate electricity. Bringing the street infrastructure into the open will help the community understand that infrastructure investments create valuable community resources.

Resilient infrastructure elements can be implemented at a range of scales, from small sites to a multi-block streetscape, to an entire neighborhood focused on a regional watershed. There are five main categories of infrastructure systems to consider.

**1. Water infrastructure includes stormwater mitigation and water conservation systems.**

Stormwater runoff is a major cause of water pollution in urban areas. Water is usually drained through engineered collection systems and discharged into nearby waterbodies, which are often polluted and unusable after rainfall. Capturing stormwater before it enters the system can increase groundwater recharge and protect aquatic habitat, resulting in cleaner and healthier watersheds. And, since most green infrastructure systems are visible and above ground, they can actively engage and educate the public about the benefits of creating environmentally friendly infrastructure systems. For example, holding water runoff in rain gardens and rain planters allows water to be cleansed through vegetation as it slowly percolates into the ground. In an urban setting, it may be most effective as part of a network of systems connected to established green spaces.

Slowing, reducing and cleaning stormwater provides additional system capacity and helps prevent sewer overflows during large storms, especially in cities with combined sewer and stormwater systems. Less water flowing through stormdrain pipes also reduces wear and tear on aging pipe infrastructure and, in the long run, saves on maintenance and replacement costs.

FACING: Inspired by Van Gogh's *Starry Night*, solar panels along a Dutch bike path power thousands of twinkling stones and LEDs. Project design and photo by Studio Roosegaarde.

RESILIENT STREETS

235

**2. Waste management systems recycle and reduce waste.** A function of our streets that many take for granted is managing material waste through garbage, recycling and composting receptacles, either permanently located or put out temporarily by residents and businesses for collection. Many cities now require that waste be sorted before collection. That will become even more important: world cities now generate 1.3 billion tons of waste a year, which will increase to an estimated 2.2 billion tons by 2025.[1] New technologies are making receptacles much more efficient. But in the developing world, there is no regular pick up and in some cities informal waste pickers supply the only waste collection. However, that may be better than non-sorted waste collection: waste pickers feed the recycling market with materials that would otherwise be dumped. A 2011 study found waste pickers retrieved 20 percent of all waste materials in cities studied. Because recycling is one of the cheapest and fastest ways to reduce GHG emissions, many municipalities are now engaging in partnerships with waste pickers, promoting source-segregation systems with membership-based organizations of waste pickers as service providers, and integrating environmental and social concerns about waste and the workforce as well.[2]

**3. Materials management systems create and source materials in a sustainable manner.** Streets offer space along the sidewalks and in medians for growing materials, which can include trees and grasses such as bamboo that act as natural fences and can also be harvested as food (bamboo shoots) or repurposed to create street furniture, for example. Beyond that,

the streets themselves can reuse materials in the asphalt (tires, plastics, roof shingles) and the concrete (photocatalytic), and reduce GHG emissions through local sourcing and manufacturing.

**4. Habitat systems conserve and develop natural habitat for wildlife.** Cities are physical barriers for wildlife movement. Adding native plants and trees into the streetscape reduces the amount of hardscape and creates additional natural habitat for animals such as native pollinators, migratory songbirds and beneficial insects. Vegetation shade reduces the urban heat island effect, lowering energy demands from nearby homes and businesses. Trees and shrubs also hold precipitation in their leaves and branches, reducing stormwater flows. Similarly, appropriate use of other planting materials, such as mulch, can help hold water and keep roots cool in plants and trees, especially in more arid climates where limiting water use is critical during warm seasons. And because they sequester carbon, plants also improve air quality.

**5. Energy management systems generate and conserve energy.** The technology is now widely available for generating power from the sun and wind—many street signs already use solar panels. And the emerging technology of kinetic energy can capture electricity generated through the weight and momentum of decelerating traffic (regenerative braking) or even people walking on a path. This distributed electricity can then be used to power streetlights, stoplights, nearby homes and businesses, and even to cool/heat roads. Streets may no longer need to be connected to the grid. This

FACING: Outdoor waste inlets in Hammarby Sjöstad, Stockholm, Sweden. Photo ©ENVAC.

can lower utility costs for local residents and businesses while providing resiliency and self-sufficiency at a street or neighborhood level, and of course working to mitigate climate change.

## GOALS

Sustainably designed streets can meet multiple goals while still maintaining the existing conveyance and delivery systems and providing complete mobility:

- Sequester carbon
- Reduce heat gain
- Generate electricity
- Conserve existing resources
- Promote economic development
- Provide habitat
- Educate community members about the societal benefit of infrastructure systems

LEFT: Dixieanne Avenue, Sacramento. Project design and photo by MIG, Inc.

**GREEN**
- Creating habitat
- Recycling
- Cleansing water
- Managing waste
- Generating energy
- Harvesting water
- Distributing materials
- Rejuvenating
- Reusing

**GROW**
- Planting
- Mulching
- Weeding
- Irrigating
- Propagating
- Pruning
- Composting
- Harvesting
- Storing

**MOVE**
- Interpreting
- Running
- Orienting
- Biking
- Parking
- Riding
- Driving
- Walking
- Servicing
- Strolling
- Navigating
- Locating
- Rolling/skating

**GATHER**
- Dancing
- Demonstrating
- People watching
- Networking
- Teaching
- Resting
- Learning
- Parading
- Eating
- Talking
- Sitting
- Playing music
- Meeting
- Singing

**SHOP**
- Selling
- Dining
- Bargaining
- Manufacturing
- Performing
- Producing
- Bartering
- Cooking
- Displaying
- Buying
- Browsing

**PLAY**
- Sensing
- Climbing
- Playing games
- Balancing
- Discovering
- Building
- Reading
- Exercising
- Drawing
- Geocaching
- Jumping
- Thinking
- Sliding

### ACTIVITIES ON RESILIENT STREETS

A new approach to our infrastructure can provide a wide range of resources, functions and materials, increasing the resiliency of our streets and cities. It can also educate the community about resiliency and promote a diversity of other street activities, in combination with all types of streets.

## 21ST STREET
*Paso Robles, California*

The street flooded—often and severely—discharging sediment directly into the Salinas River. Not to mention it had poor pavement conditions. And with fast-moving cars, it wasn't bike- or pedestrian-friendly either. Twenty-first Street is both a commercial and residential street near the Paso Robles Event Center. The street, which is one of four streets crossing railroads in town, was established decades ago in a natural drainageway.

With community input, the City decided on a new vision for five contiguous blocks of the street. The existing underground creek was daylighted, and reestablished right down the center of the street. High-volume, high-velocity water flow from the creek to the landscaped channel imitates the flow of the creek watershed, while recharging groundwater through underlying infiltration trenches and engineered mixes of soil. Riparian channel plantings and generous drought-tolerant landscape strips on both sides of the street provide a gracious public realm.

Now 26,000 square feet of pervious pavers in pedestrian areas seep up stormwater. The designers intentionally didn't install

LEFT: 21st Street, Paso Robles, California. Project design and photo by MIG, Inc.

RIGHT: 21st Street, Paso Robles, California. Project design by MIG, Inc. Photo by Cannon Corporation.

RESILIENT STREETS

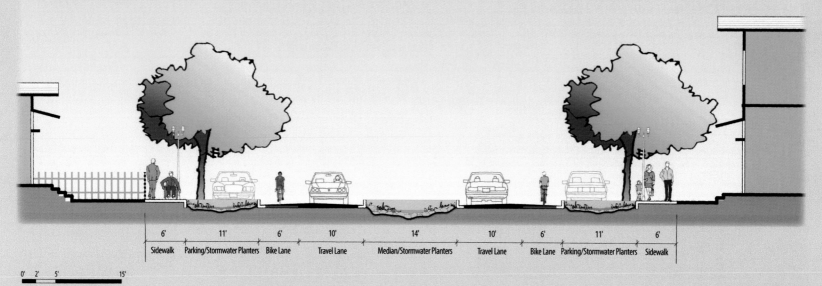

| 6' | 11' | 6' | 10' | 14' | 10' | 6' | 11' | 6' |
|---|---|---|---|---|---|---|---|---|
| Sidewalk | Parking/Stormwater Planters | Bike Lane | Travel Lane | Median/Stormwater Planters | Travel Lane | Bike Lane | Parking/Stormwater Planters | Sidewalk |

0' 2' 5' 15'

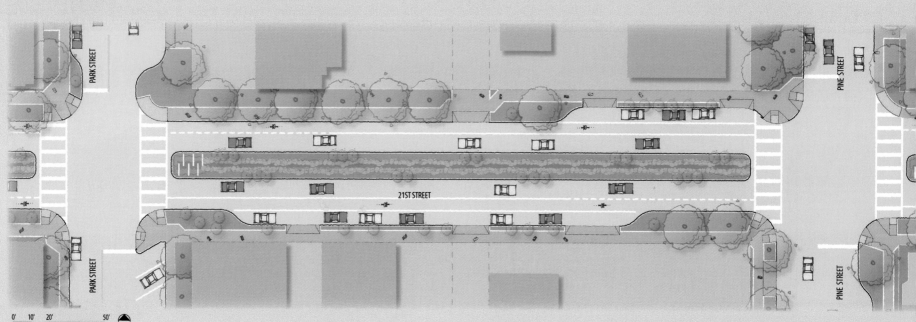

0' 10' 20' 50'

underdrains, letting the water percolate into the depressed bio-retention areas at the edge of the street. To protect those areas from unwanted subsurface water, the City installed deepened curbs, impermeable liners, and trench dams. These measures will also help keep the asphalt road dry, prolonging its lifespan.

Landscaping also has an important role. Paso Robles means "the pass of the oak trees" so all existing oaks were preserved. New native trees and plants in bio-retention areas alleviate soil erosion. And 81 new large native trees increase shade and reduce the amount of heat radiated from the pavement.

Mobility was improved by adding new marked bike lanes, crosswalks, ADA pathways, a railroad crossing and widened sidewalks. New street amenities include contemplative seating areas with Gabion basket retaining walls that use the local Adelaida stone. Bike racks and high-efficiency decorative streetlights are both functional and enhance aesthetic appeal. Finally, interpretive signs explain the entire green infrastructure system. The project cost $2.5 million, but the City received a $993,000 Urban Greening Grant to help offset costs.

RIGHT: 21st Street, Paso Robles, California. Project design by MIG, Inc. Photo by Cannon Corporation.

**What Works** Six months after completion, the 85th percentile speed had dropped 7 mph and the street had had no traffic accidents. • The street can contain a 10-year storm within the street section. • Infiltration removes the pollutants and can now treat more than 500,000 gallons of water for every rainfall over half an inch. • The open channel allows easy cleaning and visual inspection of sediment deposits. • Working with a mix of public, private, and non-governmental organizations allowed for broader support and access to innovative funding, while creating strong and diverse project advocates.

**Lessons Learned** More community education is needed about the benefits of green infrastructure and increased safety.

RESILIENT STREETS

243

# DEADERICK STREET
*Nashville, Tennessee*

It's the main physical connection between the State Legislature and the Courthouse, but the street was all concrete, filled with underutilized bus shelters, few trees. It also had a stormwater and sewage overflow problem. The three-block stretch of Deaderick Street in the central business district looked old and worn out and traffic just buzzed by. Then it was transformed into a pedestrian-friendly boulevard—the State's first green street and one of the Downtown's most livable streets.

Deaderick Street is within one of Nashville's combined storm-sewer basins and the system often overflowed into the Cumberland River. The main emphasis of the street project was to mitigate that condition. The street was reduced from four to two lanes of traffic and now incorporates three primary low-impact design elements: continuous street trees and planting zones on both sides of the street, planted bulb outs, and a central planted median. The original 30 feet of sidewalk on each side are divided into a 12–foot pedestrian area, 10-foot market zone for kiosks and an 8-foot tree-planting zone.

The facelift provided 12,000 square feet of planted areas and 5,000 square feet of porous

RESILIENT STREETS

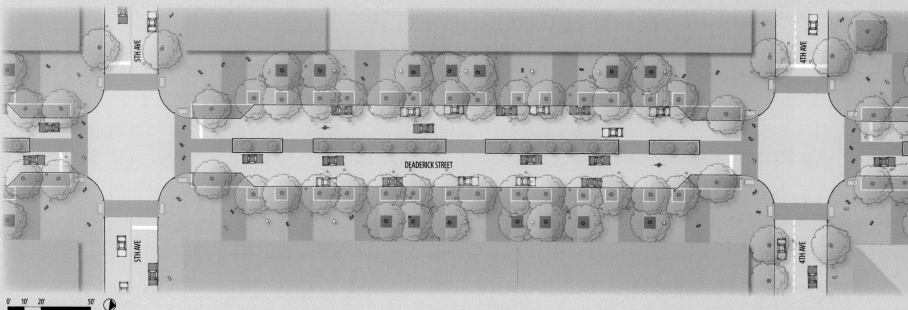

| 24' | 8' | 8' | 12' | 8' | 12' | 8' | 8' | 24' |
|-----|-----|-----|-----|-----|-----|-----|-----|-----|
| Sidewalk | Stormwater Planters | Parking | Travel Lane | Planters | Travel Lane | Parking | Stormwater Planters | Sidewalk |

0'  2'  5'  15'

DEADERICK STREET

5TH AVE

4TH AVE

0'  10'  20'  50'

concrete on the sidewalks, underlaid with structural soil that allows water to percolate down into tree root zones. Bioswales in sidewalk-level and at street-level planting areas capture, filter and infiltrate rainwater. The City planted 102 shade trees, all within 8-foot-wide rain gardens or 8x8-foot tree grates. And 53 percent of the more than 4,200 new shrubs, perennials, sedges and groundcover plants are native.

All that green infrastructure now diverts about 1.2 million gallons of stormwater away from the Cumberland River every year—with no overflow.

Continuing the green theme, the traffic signals and street lighting are now LED, there are solar-powered parking meters, bicycle storage facilities and educational kiosks that explain the benefits of urban trees, rain gardens and green infrastructure. To attract evening pedestrians, the lighted kiosks can be covered with colored films to emphasize a particular day or event such as a Titans football game or St. Patrick's Day.

Downtown workers, residents, and tourists pass beautiful plantings as they stroll along and the wide, friendly sidewalks are perfect for restaurants, cafes, vendors and kiosk tenants.

RIGHT: Photo by Hawkins Partners, Inc.

RESILIENT STREETS

247

**What Works** The facelift provided a 700% increase in pervious areas. • Native plants give the street a unique identity. • The stormwater management functions very well. • The area has been revitalized with increased numbers of businesses interested in locating there.

**Lessons Learned** Much education about green streets may be needed at all levels of the City and the community. • People had to walk a little further to get to the relocated bus stops. • One side of the street is in direct sunlight, the other shaded, which requires careful plant selection. • City ordinances may need amendments to allow for outdoor dining and restrictions on serving alcohol within the right-of-way.

# THE POLLINATOR PATHWAY
*Seattle, Washington*

Fifty percent of humans now live in urban areas. The density of our built environments, pesticide use and our penchant for planting non-native ornamental plants has led to fragmented green space and a serious decline in native pollinators (which are not honeybees, an import from Europe).

A Pollinator Pathway is a vision for a global connected ecological design that, where possible, uses streets. The project challenges us to "rebind fragmented landscapes by creating thoughtful, planned connections between green spaces."[3] It incorporates principles of ecology and design and makes specific use

of underutilized, existing infrastructure in cities. Its developer, Sarah Bergmann, says that "ecological systems in isolation don't have the resilience that connected ecology does; connecting fragmented green spaces—and the native pollinators that pollinate them— makes for a stronger ecological contribution." In Seattle, those native pollinators include hummingbirds, flies, beetles, bumblebees, mason bees, butterflies, ants and moths, all now happily flitting and pollinating on their pilot Pollinator Pathway.

The pilot, in Downtown Seattle, runs from the pesticide-free Seattle University campus

RIGHT: East Columbia Street, Seattle. Photo by MIG, Inc.

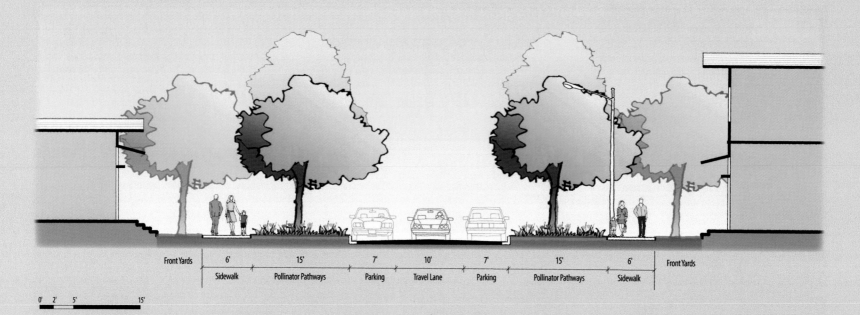

Front Yards | 6' | 15' | 7' | 10' | 7' | 15' | 6' | Front Yards
Sidewalk | Pollinator Pathways | Parking | Travel Lane | Parking | Pollinator Pathways | Sidewalk

0'  2'  5'        15'

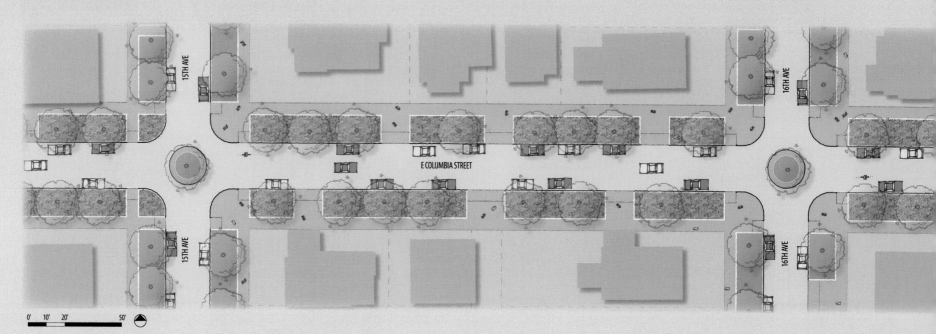

E COLUMBIA STREET

15TH AVE

16TH AVE

15TH AVE

16TH AVE

0'  10'  20'        50'

down Columbia Street to a small park with native species called Nora's Wood. It's a mile-long corridor, ranging from 4 feet to 12 feet wide, of pollinator-friendly gardens planted in the parking strips between sidewalks and street, which are technically owned by the City. There are 60 potential sites on the street, with 20 completed by the end of 2015.

A Pollinator Pathway is always a collaborative effort between participants in the project and a crew of designers, ecologists, and project managers. Plants in the project meet ecological requirements, such as 70 percent native, pollinator appeal, city requirements, drought tolerance, shade/sun and ease of care. Each garden on the project was individually designed, but with a unified design throughout the street. The rule was: make it beautiful for humans, but build it for native pollinators.

Bergmann worked with about 1,500 university students and volunteers to develop the pilot. The gardens are maintained by homeowners—who pledge not to use pesticides—and monitored by an entomologist from the Woodland Park Zoo. This is part of a larger project that visualizes a contiguous railroad of Pollinator Pathways across the continent.[4]

RIGHT: East Columbia Street, Seattle. Photo by MIG, Inc.

**What Works**  The gardens are well maintained and pesticide free. • Having one overall designer brings a design unity to the street. • It mandates collaboration with ecologists and designers. • The pathway is increasing the numbers of pollinators and the aesthetics of the street.

**Lessons Learned**  Participants need to be involved upfront to ensure they will want to and be able to maintain the garden. • Homeowners and City staff may need education about native plants and pesticides. • It is expensive to implement, so long-term grants and City funding are needed.

RESILIENT STREETS

251

# SOLAR BIKE PATH

*Krommenie, Netherlands*

If all suitable roofs in the Netherlands had solar panels, they would still only supply about 25 percent of the Dutch electricity demand. But one bike path could change everything: it has solar panels installed in the roadway. About 325 feet of a bike path in Krommenie is now an energy-harvesting solar path.[5] One side of the path is entirely solar panels; the other has small test panels for further research about surfaces.

TNO, the Dutch research company that developed SolaRoad, is working with the Province of North Holland, the construction firm Ooms Civiel, and Intech Traffic & Infra to test the path.

After one year, the roadway had stood up remarkably well to the Dutch winter and heavy bike usage—about 300,000 rides. Impressively, this one short path generated more than 9800 kWh of energy—enough to provide three households with electricity for one year. The panels are designed to last 20–25 years, similar to roof panels, and TNO estimates a payback time of 15 years.

The path was installed as prefabricated slabs, about 3 feet by 10 feet, interconnected to one another to eliminate any height differences. Each slab has a translucent top layer of tempered glass about 1 cm thick. Crystalline

RIGHT: Provincialeweg, Krommenie. Photo by SolaRoad.

RESILIENT STREETS

〉 RESILIENT STREETS

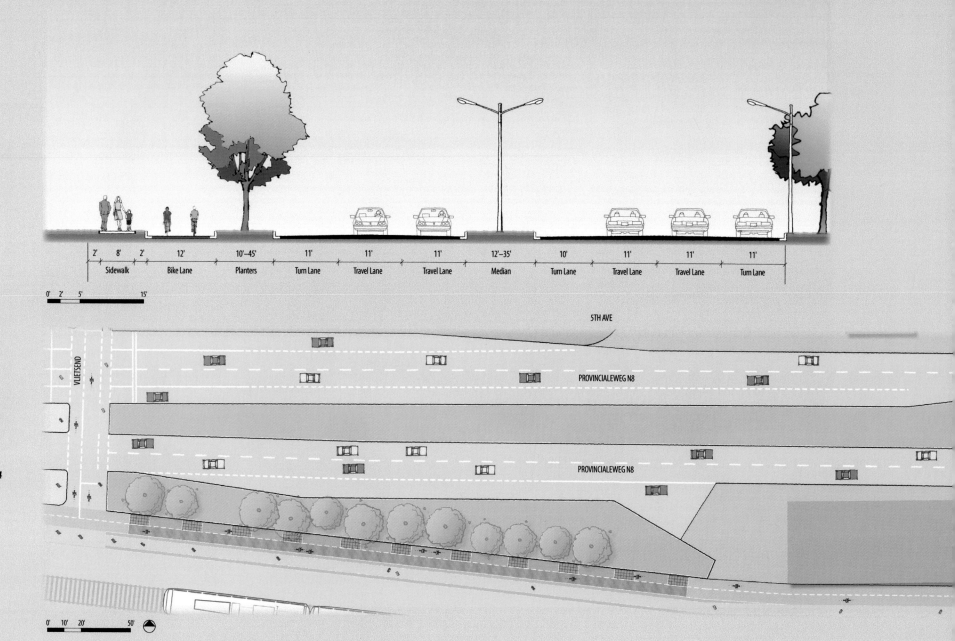

| 2' | 8' | 2' | 12' | 10'–45' | 11' | 11' | 11' | 12'–35' | 10' | 11' | 11' | 11' |
|---|---|---|---|---|---|---|---|---|---|---|---|---|
| Sidewalk | | Bike Lane | | Planters | Turn Lane | Travel Lane | Travel Lane | Median | Turn Lane | Travel Lane | Travel Lane | Turn Lane |

0'  2'  5'        15'

5TH AVE

VLIETSEND

PROVINCIALEWEG N8

PROVINCIALEWEG N8

0'  10'  20'      50'

silicon solar cells are sandwiched between that and a bottom layer of silicon rubber and concrete. The major challenge was developing a top surface that is translucent enough for sunlight to penetrate, repels as much dirt as possible, and is skid resistant and strong enough to be safe for walking, bicycling and eventually driving. A skid-resistant coating was specifically developed for the translucent layer.

The generated electrical energy is being used for road lighting and could in the future be used by nearby houses and shops, for snow melting, traffic systems, and even electric cars traveling on the road. The energy would then be generated at the place where it is needed—a big step toward energy-neutral mobility systems.

What's next? There are 140,000 kilometers of road waiting for solar in the Netherlands. And they're already talking with cities in the United States.

RIGHT: Provincialeweg, Krommenie. Photo by SolaRoad.

**What Works** The panels held up well to the elements and usage. • They generated even more energy than predicted. • There were no reported slippage or skidding accidents.

**Lessons Learned** It's expensive to manufacture and install just one pathway at a time. • Because the panels lie flat instead of pitched at the sun as on a roof, they are about 30% less efficient than roof panels.

RESILIENT STREETS

255

# PILSEN SUSTAINABLE STREET

*Chicago, Illinois*

An economic development project in the transitioning Pilsen neighborhood has resulted in what just might be the most resilient street in America.

The roads and sidewalks of this major truck corridor a few miles southwest of Downtown Chicago were in serious need of repair. The City decided to go green.[6] The street now conserves and recycles water, generates energy, provides bike lanes and seating areas, reduces heat island effects and even eats smog! Called the Pilsen Sustainable Street, it's really a two-mile section of two streets that intersect at an angle, Cermak Road and Blue Island Avenue.

The previously 20-foot-wide sidewalks were redesigned to include bike lanes and stormwater planters in parking lanes. The lanes are constructed of permeable paving blocks that allow stormwater to percolate down into the ground below. They're joined and oriented to minimize the grooves and bumps experienced by a rider passing over. And the lane blocks are blended with photocatalytic cement, a material that absorbs nitrogen oxides—a family of pollutants generated by car traffic. When sunlight hits the blocks, the pollutants are neutralized and they wash away when it rains. In other words, the path itself will be drawing pollution out of the skies and...eating it.

RESILIENT STREETS

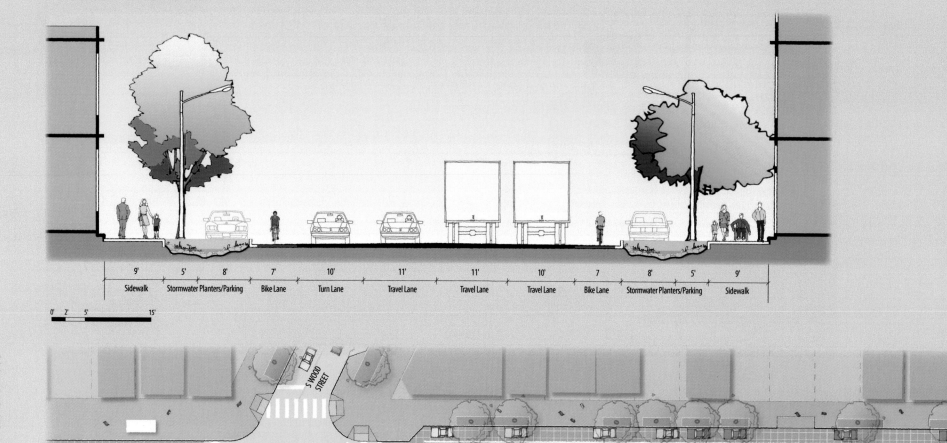

| 9' | 5' | 8' | 7' | 10' | 11' | 11' | 10' | 7 | 8' | 5' | 9' |
|---|---|---|---|---|---|---|---|---|---|---|---|
| Sidewalk | Stormwater Planters/Parking | | Bike Lane | Turn Lane | Travel Lane | Travel Lane | Travel Lane | Bike Lane | Stormwater Planters/Parking | | Sidewalk |

0'  2'  5'          15'

S WOOD STREET

S BLUE ISLAND AVENUE

S BLUE ISLAND AVENUE

0'   10'   20'        50'

The City worked with the large high school on Cermak to direct rain from its roof and paved surfaces into a water sculpture, then through a field of zeolite (which breaks down pollutants) and through a rain garden to filter out sediment and bioswales with drought-tolerant plants to trap pollutants and silt. The cleansed water ends up in the school ball field. Similar design features throughout the street divert about 80 percent of typical annual rainfall away from the combined stormwater/sewer system. No potable water is needed for irrigation.

A micro-thin concrete overlay on 40 percent of West Cermak Road reflects heat away instead of absorbing it as dark asphalt normally would. The asphalt underneath is made from recycled tires, roof shingles and aggregates.

Bus shelters use solar panels to provide electricity for illumination and hybrid streetlights have both solar panels and wind turbines to provide power—and illuminate the signage that explains the street.

The City thought green from the beginning of the construction cycle. Contractors had to document that the majority of their supplies were sourced, extracted and manufactured within 500 miles. They also had to document their waste disposal and recycling. The streetscape cost 20 percent less than the City average and it's expected to pay itself back during its lifetime.

RIGHT: West Cermak Road, Chicago. Photo by MIG, Inc.

RESILIENT STREETS

**What Works** It is changing the concept of infrastructure to place value on its social, economic and environmental benefits. • The neighborhood is now a draw for businesses and residents. • Two years of monitoring by the Metropolitan Reclamation District showed an 80% reduction in stormwater entering the stormwater/sewer system. • The street requires 42% less electricity from the grid. • It is context-sensitive: the Windy City uses wind turbines. • 23% of materials came from within 200 miles; 76% came from within 500 miles.

**Lessons Learned** Construction companies and vendors may resist documenting local purchases and using recycled content. • Construction needs to be carefully staged to minimize disruption to businesses. • Some bicyclists continue to use sidewalks.

259

LEFT: Photo by MIG, Inc.   RIGHT: Winslow Way, Bainbridge Island. Project design and photo by MIG, Inc.

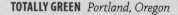 New smart technologies are emerging every day. And back-to-basics natural systems of managing water, energy, materials and habitat are becoming more common. Pair them to transform urban infrastructure and create resilient streets everywhere. Each case study provided lessons learned and became the basis for the best practices included at the end of this chapter. More information available on these and other case studies at www.reStreets.org.

### TOTALLY GREEN *Portland, Oregon*

Portland gets a *lot* of rain, which used to wash all the street dirt and pollutants into the Willamette River. But as of December 2015, 1,700 of the City's streets are now green. The City's "% for Green" program helps construct the stormwater management facilities (funded by 1 percent of the construction budget for projects requiring a street opening permit).[7] The streets reduce peak flows from their drainage areas by at least 80 percent and up to 94 percent. They also filter water to reduce total suspended solids by 90 percent, organic pollutants/oils by 90 percent and heavy metals by more than 90 percent. The bonus is that there's a 40 percent cost reduction compared to traditional pipe upsize and replacement projects. The City maintains the streets with the help of over 150 volunteer Green Street Stewards.[8]

### A FRIENDLY GREEN *Bainbridge Island, Washington*

The Bainbridge Island community took advantage of a water quality issue to recreate Winslow Way, which runs through its historic Downtown. Urban stormwater runoff was sending pollutants (bacteria, oils, heavy metals and chemicals) into Eagle Harbor and Elliott Bay. The City added stormwater planters, rain gardens and infiltration cells, along with infiltration devices that use rechargeable, self-cleaning cartridges that absorb and retain pollutants. While they were at it, the City relocated overhead utilities, improved intersections and provided wider sidewalks, gathering areas, bike facilities and site amenities. Winslow Way is now a vibrant pedestrian Downtown environment with a wide variety of activities. And water quality issues are eliminated or vastly reduced.

### HIGH FIVE, HIGH POINT *Seattle, Washington*

High Point was the first large-scale redevelopment in the US to feature low-impact, sustainable design in a dense urban setting. The development replaced aging low-income housing with hundreds of public, affordable and market rate housing units. Its narrow streets, short blocks and wide planting strips promote walking, encourage social interaction and physical activity and decrease reliance on cars. An innovative natural drainage system includes more than four miles of grass and vegetated swales, triple the number of trees and a drainage retention pond that collects and naturally cleanses about 98 percent of surface stormwater run-off, directing it into Longfellow Creek. In addition to its environmental benefits, the pond and its walking trail are a central feature and gathering place for the community.

### SMART AS A LAMPOST *Hersted, Denmark*

By day, the Hersted neighborhood of Copenhagen looks like a typical business district. But when the sun goes down it becomes a massive experiment by Danish Outdoor Lighting Lab (DOLL). Each block is testing how smart technology can transform urban infrastructure. With LED technology and sensors, lighting can be controlled and precisely managed, in milliseconds—lights brighten only when cars, bikes or people approach, and they know the difference! Lampposts collect information about climate, temperatures and street conditions, as well as driver, pedestrian and bicycle patterns. The City knows its infrastructure and capacities. Cities can use the data they collect to manage resources dynamically, save energy and increase functionality.[9]

### ONE SMALL STEP *Sydney, Australia*

The street medians and backyards in Sydney can be habitat links between existing wildlife corridors, helping animals to move through the landscape—one of the most important factors in maintaining biodiversity. Habitat Stepping Stone encourages residents to plant native flowers and plants that provide food (nectar, fruit and seeds) and add water and shelter elements (rocks, shrubs and nest boxes).[10] Information is localized to each Council District, with links to suppliers that offer special discounts. Those who pledge to add at least three elements receive a customized habitat stepping stone. The initiative was developed by the Australian Research Institute for Environment and Sustainability at Macquarie University.

261

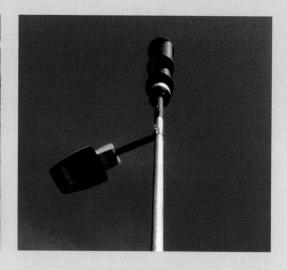

LEFT: Project design and photo by Studio Roosegaarde.  CENTER: Avenue des Champs-Élysées, Paris. Photo by Schnieder Electric.  RIGHT: Noordforce.com

### A STARRY NIGHT *Eindhoven, Netherlands*

When the sun goes down, this bike path allows you to walk or cycle right through Vincent Van Gogh's beautiful and iconic "Starry Night." Solar panels along the path harvest energy during the day and power the thousands of twinkling stones and LEDs that form swirls of stars. Special paint also charges during the day and glows all night. Each illuminated fleck acts like a small brushstroke, adding a tiny but crucial element to the swirling whole. People bike from miles away to ride on the 1-kilometer path, developed by Rotterdam-based Daan Roosegaard and Heijmans Infrastructure.

### ENERGY, STEP-BY-STEP *Paris, France*

As they ran along Avenue des Champs Élysée, marathoners thumped on 176 special tiles for 25 meters and generated enough electricity to power a light bulb for 40 days and 40 nights. The energy-harvesting tiles were developed by London-based Pavegen Systems. They're made of recycled polymer with a top surface of recycled truck tires. The surface flexes about five millimeters when stepped on, which creates kinetic energy that is then converted to produce about 6 watts per step. They're designed to be installed in areas with high foot traffic, to power shops, streetlights, signage and advertising displays. They can also be used to power off-the-grid urban communities in the developing world—Pavegen has pilots in several of Rio de Janeiro's favelas and has installed the tiles in areas worldwide, including DuPont Circle, Washington, DC.

### RUN LIKE THE WIND *Juist, Germany*

This island in the North Sea, off Germany's northern coast, is noted for wind; sun, not so much. Wind turbine-powered LED street lamps are a clear solution for areas where there isn't enough sun to power solar cells. Wahlstedt, Germany-based Noordforce developed a wind generator with lithium batteries that are fully charged after a half day of moderate winds and don't need recharging for 10 days. The lights run off the batteries. Because the lights are not connected to a power grid they can be installed in more remote places like Juist, and along bus stops, bike and footpaths between villages and small settlements.[11]

### HEAT ON THE STREET  *Waarland, Netherlands*

A Dutch company has found a way to use some of the heat and cold that black asphalt roads naturally store. Ooms Civiel's Road Energy System runs water through a maze of small pipes under the asphalt that is then heated from the warmth of the road. The heated water is then sent to nearby houses, and can be pulled up to prevent ice from building up on the road during winter months. A test of just 200 yards generated enough heat for 70 apartments in a four-story building.[12] A real-life application in Waarland, Netherlands, combines the system with a housing project: 35 houses use the heating and cooling system, which also serves as an energy supplier for the entire neighborhood.

### GREEN PRIDE  *Sacramento, California*

Dixieanne Avenue, which connects a multimodal light rail station to a North Sacramento neighborhood park, was aging and unappealing to walk or ride through, especially at night. It drained directly into the American River. To improve water quality and enhance the identity of the street, the six-block streetscape improvements include tree-lined sidewalks, class III bike facilities and iconic art that reflects the community's values. The key was to minimize impervious surfaces and urban runoff with stormwater planters along separated sidewalks, bioswales in midblock bulb outs, pervious paving in the traffic circle and a pocket plaza—with a context-sensitive planting palette. Cars, pedestrians and bicyclists now share the road, which has become a great source of community pride as its neighborhood "main street."

### ART AND LIGHT  *Jerusalem, Israel*

When all is still, they're closed up like giant, sleeping red poppies. But when it senses a person or tram approach, poppy petals burst open and light up. During the day, they also provide shelter from the sun and rain. The installation of two sets of 30-feet high poppies on either side of a tramline detects motion, which then triggers the petals to inflate to about 30 feet wide each. They're installed in Jerusalem's Valero Square, a previously underutilized and neglected area in the center of Downtown. While thousands moved through the square on a daily basis, virtually no one stopped to spend time in it. The installation has created a more playful, interactive environment, which has invited people to linger and actively engage with it.

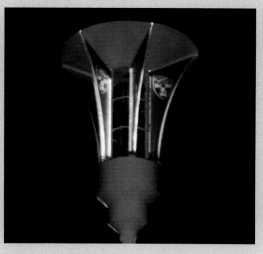

**FEEL THE HEAT**  *Toulouse, France*

Lights at night are at half strength in Toulouse—until someone walks near a lamppost. The posts detect human body heat and immediately double their illumination. Ten seconds later they revert to normal (and the next post in the pathway lights up). The aim is to cut energy consumption by 50 percent, first on the 550-yard section of a busy street on which it's installed and eventually throughout the City of 450,000 people. And an added benefit is reducing light pollution in the night sky so people can see the stars again.

**ZAP IT!**  *Kuala Lumpur, Malaysia*

Eight LED street lamps in Kuala Lumpur incorporate both a solar panel and a wind turbine—and they zap mosquitos too! Mosquitos are attracted to very small amounts of carbon dioxide the lamps emit, the same gas that humans give off. The insects are most active at dusk, just when the lamps come on, and they get sucked into a capture net. The Eco-Greenergy lighting system was developed at the University of Malaya, designed to help fight dengue fever. The mosquito-borne viral disease has increased by 30 times in the past 50 years, with Malaysia especially hard hit. Since the light is off the electrical grid, it's perfect for remote areas. At $2,800 to buy and install, the lamps are still relatively expensive, but with demand the price could decrease.[13]

**FRUITS OF THE STREET**  *Davis, California*

In the autumn, walkers on Olive Drive need to keep their eyes on the ground—the fruity olives will be dropping from the trees and staining the sidewalks a deep purple. Despite its location near Downtown and busy traffic corridors, the mature olive trees give the street a small town atmosphere. Residents and nearby UC Davis staff harvest the crop and undertake the long treatment process that makes them edible. In fact, the UC Davis Olive Center bottles and sells a line of olive oil from these trees, mixed with the fruit of trees on campus and nearby groves. The Olive Center aims to do for olives what UC Davis has already done for the world-renowned California wine industry.[14]

**SUSTAINABLE BRIDGE** *Leiyang, China*

This bridge can support 16-ton trucks—and it's made of sustainable bamboo. Engineers cut strips from large stalks, arranged them in multiple layers and bonded them with proprietary glue and weatherproofing. Bamboo is actually stronger than steel when stretched and more robust than concrete when compressed. While producing concrete emits 5–10 percent of global $CO_2$, bamboo soaks up and sequesters $CO_2$ forever. Stalks mature in just a few years, much faster than trees, and are mowed like grass, leaving their roots intact to grow again. The bridge is about 32 feet long, but engineers say that, based on structural testing, 100-feet long bamboo bridges are certainly feasible and they could support even heavier loads. The bridge was a joint development of the University of Southern California and Hunan University in China.[15]

**PLASTIC ROADS** *Vancouver, Canada*

The asphalt on the road looks and feels familiar, but it's actually asphalt mixed with synthetic wax from post-consumer recycled plastics like milk jugs and shampoo bottles. In 2012, Vancouver became the first City to use the wax, developed by GreenMantra Technologies. It allows a "warm mix" paving process—the asphalt can be produced and transported at 250°F instead of 320°F. That results in about 20 percent energy savings and lower emissions both at the plants that produce asphalt and from the trucks that deliver it. The wax also allows more recycled asphalt to be used in the roads, without affecting performance. The City and GreenMantra are still studying and improving on ways to produce even "greener" roads—they are now experimenting with blending in soy wax, which could reduce temperatures even further.

**UNDERGROUND TRASHY** *Kitchener, Ontario, Canada*

Why not extend trashcans below ground? Molok® receptacles, developed in Finland, are 60 percent below ground, making them much larger than standard trashcans so they have to be emptied much less often. The City of Kitchener used to collect trash every day. Now they collect three times a week. While the City increased its Downtown public events and festivals, the units have been able to meet the needs of the event goers without having to place additional portable containers on the street. The design also benefits from the laws of nature: gravity compacts the waste, which further increases capacity, and the cooler temperatures underground slow bacterial development, reducing odors and pests. They're emptied by pulling up a reusable liner and opening the bottom of the liner, which keeps the main container clean.

LEFT: Photo by Yan Xiao, Ph.D. CENTER: Kingsway, Vancouver. Photo by Brian Soland/MIG, Inc. RIGHT: Photo by Molok North America Ltd.

RESILIENT STREETS

265

Integrating bioswales, raingardens and stormwater planters helps cleanse and harvest rain, while adding aesthetic value. Installing solar, wind and kinetic energy-producing elements takes a street to the next level of generating its own energy and providing opportunities for community education as well.

## Bioswales and rain gardens

These shallow vegetated channels have sloped sides and provide treatment and retention as they either move stormwater down the street, or collect and naturally cleanse runoff, letting it percolate into groundwater.

## Furniture

Fixed and movable tables and seating—made of recycled materials that are durable and require minimal maintenance—provide functional surfaces.

## Lighting

Lighting is important for nighttime visibility and a sense of security. It can be provided through renewably generated power, using fixtures that can cut energy consumption by illuminating only when needed.

## Mulch

Mulch holds water from rain and irrigation, reducing the amount of water required to maintain trees and vegetation.

## Paving

A variety of paving types, including permeable pavement—which lets water percolate into the ground—can differentiate areas from roadway paving, providing safety surfacing and visual interest.

## Photocatalytic materials

"Smog-eating" materials in sidewalks and roadways can reduce the nitrogen oxides generated by cars.

## Structures

Arbors, pergolas, canopies and tents can be made from solar arrays and recycled materials to protect people from harsh weather, while generating energy.

## Trash and recycling receptacles

Separate containers for trash and different types of recycling and composting are essential for maintaining cleanliness. New technology can expand receptacle efficiency.

## Trees

Trees reduce the urban heat gain, hold carbon, provide shade and habitat for birds and people; trees like coconut, palm and bamboo produce useful materials.

## Vegetation

Vegetated areas provide food and habitat pathways for pollinators and can hold and cleanse rainwater.

### Geothermal pipes

Water pipes under streets and sidewalks can take advantage of underground heat during winter to melt snow and heat nearby buildings.

### Interpretive art and signage

Placed on or near sustainable infrastructure systems, art and visually appealing signage can help community members understand how their city uses green infrastructure.

### Irrigation

Water-efficient drip irrigation systems and smart controllers reduce water requirements.

### Kinetic energy structures

Kinetic power installations can collect energy from cars or people to use for street lighting and other electrical needs, while adding visual and educational value.

### Rainwater harvesting structures

Surface and subsurface stormwater storage structures such as rain barrels and cisterns can retain stormwater and allow it to be available for future landscaping use.

### Recycled materials

Furniture, pavement and other elements can be constructed from recycled materials including plastic, wood and metal.

### Solar tiles

Small tiles can be used to provide lighting for a single sign or bus shelter; larger systems can generate electricity to power street lighting and other electrical needs on sections of the street.

### Stormwater planters

Planter boxes are small rain gardens with vertical walls that collect and absorb runoff. They're ideal for space-limited sites in denser urban areas.

### Water source

Non-potable water for cleaning the physical environment and watering vegetation can come from rain barrels and cisterns.

### Windmills/turbines

Structures to capture wind power can provide electricity and add visual interest.

# CREATING A RESILIENT STREET

One day, it just might be possible for all streets to be resilient, off the grid, generating energy for their own lighting (and perhaps for the business and homes alongside them), managing and harvesting stormwater, melting snow, offering linked plots of habitat, while still accommodating vehicles, bicycles and people. But, for now, take an incremental approach. Tackle one section of one street at a time and let the combination of elements build over time. Implementing these best practices can help create resilient streets.

Because new infrastructure technology is constantly emerging, new best practices will also be developed. Check the website—reStreets.org—for new case studies and updated best practices. And please post examples of how your community is creating resilient streets so others can benefit from them too.

# Take a comprehensive approach to conservation design

**1** Identify opportunities to include all five types of sustainable infrastructure systems (water, habitat, energy, materials and waste).

**2** Design for a low carbon footprint for both new improvements and long-term maintenance.

**3** Identify, protect and link critical ecological corridors in advance of streetscape improvements.

**4** Minimize demolition and use of new materials where feasible.

**5** Encourage new construction supplies and streetscape furnishings to be sourced, extracted and manufactured locally.

**6** Size impervious roadway lane widths to minimize total runoff and maximize opportunities for pervious surfaces.

**7** Maximize multiuse, multipurpose elements. Appropriate multiuse vertical elements include pedestrian lights with solar panels and wind turbines that generate energy, and parking lanes that serve as stormwater planters.

**8** Preserve, where possible, existing open spaces and tree cover to provide areas where water can infiltrate or evaporate.

**9** Use green infrastructure to improve safety and overall experience for all users. Traffic-calming features such as tree-lined medians, landscaped bulb outs and traffic circles also serve as desirable locations for green infrastructure. Use LED street lights and guidance signs powered by solar and wind energy.

## Encourage low-impact and pollinator-friendly landscaping

**1** Provide low-impact vegetation to control and improve stormwater, increase water infiltration, minimize water usage, reduce heat island effects, and add value and beauty to the street right-of-way.

**2** Plant native and non-native plants with deep root growth and pest resistance to improve long-term viability of the plants, while minimizing maintenance costs.

**3** Encourage a mix of native plants and ornamental plants to enhance diversity.

**4** Select drought-resilient plants, especially in communities with low precipitation and constrained water resources.

**5** Minimize plant waste by fertilizing, irrigating and pruning judiciously, recycling grass and mulching and composting plant debris.

**5** Nurture soil and biodiversity by minimizing pesticides and chemicals that harm beneficial soil organisms. Protect soils from compaction and erosion and replenish soil by using organic matter, mulching and slow-release organic fertilizers.

**7** Plant pollinator-friendly plants that attract pollinators such as hummingbirds, flies, beetles, bees and butterflies.

**8** Provide habitat links between existing wildlife corridors by integrating food, water, shelter and nesting elements within existing planting strips and incorporating native flowers, shrubs, rocks and nest boxes.

RESILIENT STREETS

271

## Integrate stormwater systems

**1** Maximize tree cover and pervious surfaces to reduce stormwater runoff and overall heat gain.

**2** Provide opportunities to maximize tree roots in constrained areas by using structural soil, silva cells, etc., around tree planter areas.

**3** Replace solid coverage of asphalt or concrete with pervious asphalt, pervious concrete, permeable pavers, and plastic grid systems to allow water infiltration to tree root zones.

**4** Maximize natural landscaped methods of handling stormwater to reduce the need for constructing large control devices.

**5** Use a watershed approach to determine the best locations within a drainage area for stormwater improvements such as stormwater planters, bioswales, flow-through planters, pervious pavers, etc.

**6** Locate landscape stormwater solutions in medians, planting areas next to sidewalks, and in traffic-calming features such as traffic circles and curb extensions at intersections and between intersections.

**7** Explore large water storage vaults under impervious drive lanes and parking lanes to capture rainwater funneled from surrounding impervious areas.

**8** Include filter strips beside paved areas to slow the flow of stormwater and reduce the volume of runoff.

## Harvest and reuse graywater

**1** Harvest rainwater for irrigation and to assist in water quality protection.

**2** Use rain barrels and cisterns—above or below ground—to collect rainwater.

**3** Release the collected stormwater stored in rain barrels and cisterns very slowly into stormwater planters or directly into soil.

**4** Ensure that all water storage containers are covered to prevent mosquito breeding and to reduce evaporation losses, contamination and algal growth.

**5** Calculate the irrigation needs of various plants to match the amount of graywater that is needed, amount of rainwater that needs to be harvested, and the short-term and long-term storage required during different seasons of the year.

**6** Use drip irrigation for watering plants. Where possible, use gravity pressure or pumps to supply water from the storage system.

**7** Partner with adjoining property owners to source different types of graywater from laundry, kitchen sinks and showers.

**8** Use simple graywater systems for specific, large plants such as trees, bushes, berry patches, shrubs, and large annuals. Avoid the use of graywater to irrigate small plants that are spread over large areas like flower beds.

**9** Design graywater systems for the water to soak directly into the ground. Calculate infiltration and soil percolation rates of the soil to ensure that graywater infiltrates into the ground. Minimize all direct contact and ensure that graywater is not available for people or animals to drink. Avoid pooling or graywater run off.

**10** Do not store graywater for more than 24 hours to prevent nutrient decay and bad odors.

**11** Monitor pH and chemical readings to prevent damage to plants.

**12** Clean and regularly maintain rainwater harvesting and graywater systems to keep the system hygienic.

## Integrate solar and wind energy systems

**1** Install solar and wind energy generating elements in the street ROW to serve essential street operations such as street lighting, traffic signalization and irrigation, as well as to provide additional amenities such as powering decorative lighting, special events, charging stations for smart phones, etc.

**2** Integrate vertical solar and wind-based energy elements in common streetscape elements such as traffic signals, street lights, pedestrian lights, parking meters, bus shelters, etc.

**3** Integrate horizontal solar panels in multimodal facilities such as bike lanes and pedestrian sidewalks.

**4** Design dynamic solar arrays in shade structures and pergolas. Movable solar panels can change their orientation throughout the day to follow the sun's path and maximize solar energy generation.

**5** Design solar and wind generating elements as iconic gateways, interactive art features, etc.

**6** Partner with adjoining uses such as buildings and open spaces to increase opportunities for wind and solar energy generation, minimizing impacts such as shade on solar panels. Incorporate vertical solar panels in front of blank walls and building elevations.

**7** Ensure that horizontal solar panels along sidewalks and bike facilities are skid-resistant.

**8** Ensure that horizontal solar and wind energy generating installations are ADA compliant in terms of vertical and horizontal clearances.

**9** Mitigate energy generation impacts to migratory birds and pollinators. Mitigate heat and glare impacts of solar panels.

**10** Ensure that the utility boxes associated with wind and solar energy generation, such as battery storage boxes, do not affect the overall function and aesthetics of the street.

**11** Use interactive display panels and signage to provide "real time" tracking of energy generation.

## Harvest kinetic energy

(1) Locate different types of kinetic energy generators in both roadways and sidewalks to illuminate street lights, minor plazas, etc.

(2) Install kinetic energy collectors at transit stops where buses and trains are braking heavily.

(3) Install kinetic energy collectors at railroad crossings to harvest energy from passing trains.

(4) Install kinetic collectors at traffic-calming devices such as speed bumps and raised crosswalks and intersections.

(5) Install kinetic energy collectors in well-used pedestrian sidewalks and walkways to major transit stations, public and private destinations such as civic centers, convention centers, grocery stores, etc.

(6) Ensure that kinetic energy generators in sidewalks and walkways are skid-resistant and ADA compliant.

(7) Ensure that the utility boxes associated with kinetic energy generation, such as battery storage boxes, do not affect the overall function and aesthetics of the street.

(8) Use interactive display panels and signage to provide "real time" tracking of energy generation.

# Reduce pollution, energy consumption and waste materials

(1) Use streetscape furnishings and paving surfaces to reduce energy consumption and waste materials and minimize air and light pollution and landfill.

(2) Install LED technology in street lights, traffic signals and guidance signs to reduce power consumption.

(3) Integrate LED dimming technologies to lower or turn off lights during periods of inactivity.

(4) Customize outdoor street lighting codes to meet the unique needs of individual communities.

(5) Allow dark sky-friendly street lighting systems to balance light pollution with public safety by lighting places appropriately when needed, no brighter than necessary and fully shielded to avoid unnecessary glare.

(6) Integrate energy conserving street lights that generally illuminate at half strength until human body heat and motion detection transform them to normal illumination.

(7) Explore non-electric elements in paving surfaces such as special paint that charges during the day and glows all night.

(8) Provide energy systems under asphalt roads to use the naturally stored cold and heat to prevent ice from building up on roads.

(9) Provide micro-thin concrete overlays on traditional asphalt roadways to minimize typical heat gain of dark asphalt.

(10) Incorporate photocatalytic cement into roadways and walkways to absorb nitrogen oxide, a key pollutant emitted by cars.

(11) Encourage "below ground" waste containers that use gravity to compact waste to increase capacity and slow bacterial development to reduce odors and pests.

(12) Use "smart" waste systems that incorporate real time and historical collection data to shrink collection frequency, while increasing opportunities to recycle and compost.

## Harvest and recycle materials

(1) Grow emerging building materials such as bamboo along medians and planting strips.

(2) Recycle on-site and off-site materials in paving surfaces and street furnishings to minimize landfill and the high cost of disposing old materials.

(3) Transplant and reuse mature trees such as live oaks.

(4) Recycle old materials in innovative ways such as curbs as seating walls, dumpster sides as street furniture and parking meters as bicycle racks.

(5) Experiment with low energy-intensive and carbon sequestering materials, such as repurposed bamboo, to replace energy-intensive concrete.

(6) Use asphalt that is made from recycled materials such as tires, roofs and shingles and aggregates.

(7) Encourage cities, designers and contractors to embrace new technologies.

(8) When recycling on-site materials, carefully stage construction to minimize disruption to existing businesses.

# Integrate art and signage

LEFT: Grange Avenue, Greendale, Wisconsin. Photo by Aaron Volkening. Licensed under Creative Commons 2.0. RIGHT: Rain Garden at the corner of First and Kingsley, Ann Arbor, Michigan. Sculpture by Joshua Wiener; Photo by Sharon VanderKaay. Licensed under Creative Commons 2.0.

**1** Use art and interactive signage to educate community members about green infrastructure.

**2** Locate large art and signage features in highly visible and known community gathering spaces, transit stops and other similar locations.

**3** Install smaller art and interpretive elements on the street and planting areas that explain the benefits of green infrastructure.

**4** Design solar panels in paving surfaces to create playful "checkerboard" layouts to engage and attract multigenerational audiences.

**5** Use stormwater collection systems in an engaging and fun way to educate the public.

**6** Mark the myriad lines of different underground utilities in different colors to create distinctive roadway paving patterns that also showcase the complex network of wet and dry utilities.

**7** Install art and light systems that use renewable energy.

# Encourage community participation

**1** Form public/private partnerships to involve community members in project design, construction and maintenance.

**2** Build partnerships with schools so that students can learn about green infrastructure and its relevance and importance in serving their community.

**3** Provide incentives such as tax credits to encourage green infrastructure systems.

**4** Provide incentives for integrated green infrastructure systems in adjoining residential and commercial developments.

**5** Implement "adopt a median" and "adopt a stormwater planter" to encourage regular maintenance.

**6** Educate community members on the benefits of green infrastructure systems and the technological advancements now available.

RESILIENT STREETS

279

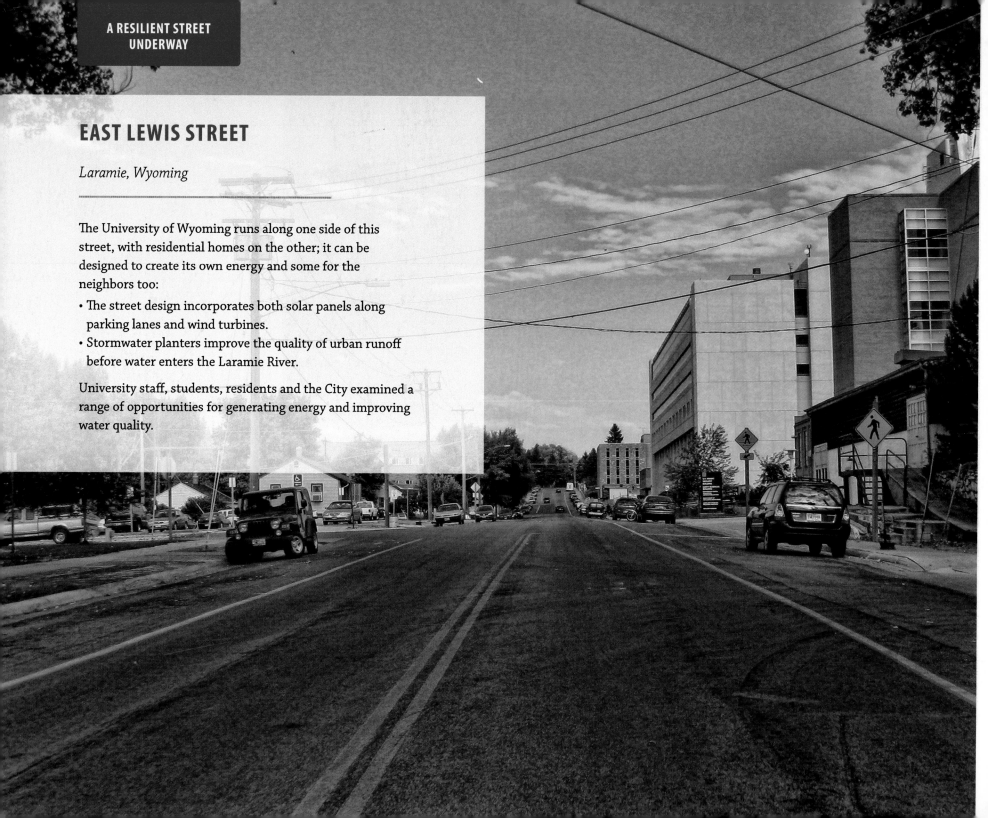

## EAST LEWIS STREET

*Laramie, Wyoming*

The University of Wyoming runs along one side of this street, with residential homes on the other; it can be designed to create its own energy and some for the neighbors too:

• The street design incorporates both solar panels along parking lanes and wind turbines.
• Stormwater planters improve the quality of urban runoff before water enters the Laramie River.

University staff, students, residents and the City examined a range of opportunities for generating energy and improving water quality.

## CHAPTER 1: THE WORLD ON THE STREET

**1.** Louise Dawson, "How the bicycle became the symbol of women's emancipation," in The Guardian, November 4, 2011, accessed at theguardian.com/environment/bike-blog/2011/nov/04/bicycle-symbol-womens-emancipation.

**2.** As recently as 1965, the world's production of cars and bikes was essentially the same, with each at nearly 20 million. As of 2003, bike production had climbed to over 100 million per year compared with 42 million cars. Bicycle production was 105 million units globally in 2004, a 1.5 percent increase over 2003, according to WorldWatch Institute. More information available at worldometers.info/bicycles.

**3.** This quote is attributed to Gottlieb Daimler, inventor of the gas-powered motorcar, in 1889. However, it's also been attributed to a "spokesperson" for Daimler-Benz, so it may be apocryphal. Nonetheless, it reflects society's thoughts about motorcars versus horses at that time.

**4.** U.S. Department of Transportation, Bureau of Transportation Statistics Publications, "National Transportation Statistics," Table 1-40: U.S. Passenger Miles. Retrieved June 2015.

**5.** Donald Shoup, "The High Cost of Free Parking," published by the American Planning Association, 2005. More information also at reinventingparking.org.

**6.** The World Factbook, Central Intelligence Agency.

**7.** J. Barry Cullingworth, Editor, Energy, Land and Public Policy. Transaction Publishers, 1990.

**8.** "2010 Annual Urban Mobility Report," published by the Transportation Institute at Texas A&M University. The Institute analyzed traffic congestion in 439 U.S. urban areas. Updated reports available at mobility.tamu.edu/ums/report.

**9.** Noted in two reports by the Governors Highway Safety Association, "Spotlight on Highway Safety: Bicyclist Safety," and "Spotlight on Highway Safety: Pedestrian Fatalities by State," both published in October 2014.

**10.** An analysis by Transportation for America documented in "2011 Dangerous by Design, Solving the Epidemic of Preventable Pedestrian Deaths, of the National Highway Traffic Safety Administration's Fatality Analysis Reporting System" shows that 52 percent of all pedestrian deaths were on principal or minor arterials and 60 percent of pedestrian deaths were on roads with speeds of 40 miles per hour or higher.

**11.** In "Streetwise," The Economist, September 5, 2015, accessed at economist.com/news/international/21663219-cities-are-starting-put-pedestrians-and-cyclists-motorists-makes-them?frsc=dg percent7Cc.

**12.** Heidi Garrett-Peltier, "Estimating the Employment Impacts of Pedestrian, bicycle and road infrastructure, Case Study – Baltimore", shows that road construction jobs create approximately 7 jobs per $1 million spending, pedestrian projects create over 11 jobs for the same level of spending, and bicycle projects create up to 14 jobs.

13. More information about highway systems and the CSS report is available on the Institute of Transportation Engineers website at ite.org/css and on the U.S. Department of Transportation website at flh.fhwa.dot.gov/about/css and at ContextSensitiveSolutions.org

14. From a study by transport scholar Noreen McDonald of the University of North Carolina, "Are Millennials Really the 'Go-Nowhere' Generation?" in the Journal of the American Planning Association, Vol. 81, Issue 2, 2015.

15. Tony Dutzik and Jeff Inglis (Frontier Group) and Phineas Baxandall, Ph.D. (U.S. PIRG Education Fund), "Millennials in Motion: Changing Travel Habits of Young Americans and the Implications for Public Policy," U.S. PIRG Education Fund and Frontier Group. October 2014. Accessed at uspirg.org/reports/usp/millennials-motion.

16. General Motors Chief Executive Officer Mary Barra, during a presentation to investors and journalists, December 2017.

17. M. Bart Herring, Director of Product Management, Mercedes-Benz USA.

18. "Experts" haven't always been the best at predictions: "That the automobile has practically reached the limit of its development is suggested by the fact that during the past year no improvements of a radical nature have been introduced," from *Scientific American,* Jan 2, 1909.

19. A study conducted by the U.S. Department of Transportation, Federal Highway Administration, Office of Highway Policy Information, accessed at fhwa.dot.gov/policyinformation/statistics/2013/vmt422c.cfm.

20. Susan Goltsman, FASLA, a founding principal of MIG, Inc., was an internationally recognized expert in designing inclusive environments. Her work established new relationships between the environment and healthy human development. Her vision is reflected in the content of the "Play" chapter.

### CHAPTER 3: MOVE ALONG THE STREET

1. The American Association of State Highway and Transportation Officials model. More information about federal roadway classifications available at fhwa.dot.gov and at www.transportation.org.

2. Quoted by Tom McNichol in "Roads Gone Wild," *Wired Magazine*, December 2004. Monderman is the guru of the "Naked Streets" movement.

3. "MIT Research: Brain Processing of Visual Information," MIT news Office, December 1996. Accessed at http://news.mit.edu/1996/visualprocessing.

4. Robert E. Jacobson, ed. *Information Design*, The MIT Press, Cambridge Massachusetts, 1999.

5. The study was conducted by the Wiltshire County Council between 1997 and 2003, available at apbp.org/resource/resmgr/files/wiltshire_county_council_cen.pdf.

6. More information about smell and wayfinding in Constance Classen, David Howes, and Anthony Synnott. Introduction. Aroma: the Cultural History of Smell. London: Routledge, 1994. 1-2.

7. Yi-Fu Tuan. *Space and Place: The Perspective of Experience*. University of Minnesota Press. 2001.

8. An article by Christopher McCahill and Norman Garrick in Urban Design International, 17, 221–227 (Autum 2012), "Automobile Use and Land Consumption, Empirical Evidence from 12 Cities," examined cities during a 50-year period. They made the case that while cities with minimum parking requirements had intended to support economic development by making it easy to park downtown, the results were the opposite. As cities gave more and more land to parking (in New Haven, Connecticut as much as 20 percent of the downtown is taken up by parking), the number of people and jobs dropped by as much as 15 percent and median family incomes fell by 20 percent. Cities that instead limited parking realized denser downtowns with more jobs, more people and higher incomes.

McCahill followed up on that study with an epidemiologically based study presented at the 2016 Transportation Research Board Conference. Examining the area devoted to parking in nine cities, they found direct causality: when parking spots per building area increased, the mode share for driving increased, even approaching 100%.

9. Ricardo Olea, "San Francisco's Octavia Boulevard," San Francisco Municipal Transportation Agency, accessed at westernite.org/annualmeetings/sanfran10/Papers/Session%202_Papers/ITE%20Paper_2B-Olea.pdf.

10. For more information about circulation in the larger Central Freeway-Octavia-Market Street area, see the final report at sfcta.org/octaviacirculation.

11. For more information about the Hemisfair site, visit hemisfair.org. For a historical look, visit worldsfair68.info.

12. More information about Pottstown and other cities is available at streetsblog.org/2008/01/03/the-case-against-pull-in-angle-parking (click on the link to the Nelson\Nygaard Consulting Associates report, "Back-in/Head-Out Angle Parking").

13. "Københavns Kommunes Evaluering af Nørrebrogadeprojektets Etape 1," accessed at copenhagenize.com/2013/02/nrrebrogade-car-freeish-success.html. Also, more information about Copenhagen's bicycle strategy is in "Good, Better, Best," published by the City of Copenhagen, available at www.kk.dk/cityofcyclists.

**14.** Mike Goodno, "Cycle Tracks and Green Lanes in Washington, DC," District Department of Transportation, March 19, 2013. More information at ddot.dc.gov/page/bicycle-lanes.

**15.** Jack Ahern, "Landscape Architecture Study Tour," published by the Department of Landscape Architecture and Regional Planning, University of Massachusetts, Amherst, 2010. More technical information available in "Changing the Residential Street Scene," by Eran Ben-Joseph, in the APA Journal, Autumn 1995.

**16.** Department for Transportation (2005) "Home Zones: Challenging the Future of Our Streets," London DfT.

Gill, Tim (2006) "Lessons from London Play's Home Zones project Report."

The UK Department for Transport (http://www.dft.gov.uk/).

Sustrans "What is DIY Streets?" (http://www.sustrans.org.uk/what-we-do/liveable-neighbourhoods/diy-streets).

**17.** Department for Transportation (2005) "Home Zones: Challenging the Future of Our Streets," London DfT; also "Lessons from London Play's Home Zones Project Report," by Tim Gill, 2006.

## CHAPTER 4: GATHER ON THE STREET

**1.** Donald Appleyard, *Livable Streets*. Berkeley: University of California Press; 1981.

**2.** Allan B. Jacobs, *Great Streets*. Boston: Massachusetts Institute of Technology, 1993.

**3.** More information at www.cityrepair.org.

**4.** Semenza, Jan C., PhD, MPH, MS, "The Intersection of Urban Planning, Art and Public Health: The Sunnyside Piazza," American Journal of Public Health, September 2003.

**5.** Andres Power, San Francisco Planning Department, Urban Design Group, P2P Project Manager (former), Interview.

**6.** San Francisco Planning Department, "San Francisco Parklet Manual," available at pavementtoparks.sfplanning.org.

**7.** Accessed at http://universitycity.org/blog/ucd-releases-report-parklets.

**8.** John King, "How S.F.'s Parklet Movement Has Grown Across the Globe," San Francisco Chronicle, March 30, 2015.

**9.** More information at raahgiriday.com and embarqindiahub.org/Data/videos.

**10.** "Under the hood" code, music files and graphics are available at github.com/ohheckyeah.

11. More information at nianticlabs.com and wired. com/2015/09/pokemon-go-mobile. Other augmented reality under development includes Microsoft Hololens and Magic Leap.

12. Philadelphia's tour game is available at VisitPhilly.com/ newamericans in English, Spanish, Chinese and French. Get *your* game on at Klikaklu.com, GooseChase.com, Scavify.com or StrayBoots.com. There are likely many more!

13. Interview with OhHeckYeah founder Brian Corrigan, June 2015. OhHeckYeah is a public benefit corporation. OhHeckYeah.com.

14. According to Crashstat.org.

15. Green Light for Midtown Evaluation, New York Department of Transportation, 2010.

16. Little Italy Association, littleitalysd.com.

17. Piazza Basilone, http://www.littleitalysd.com/points-of-interest/piazza-basilone/.

18. Paul Shigley, "In Shadows Of Downtown, SD's Little Italy Thrives Again," October 29 2008, accessed at cp-dr. com/node/2169.

19. More information about the night market at garfieldnightmarket.org and Penn Avenue Unblurred at pennavenue.org.

20. You'll find kits for creating inviting front yards at friendlyfronts.com.

21. William Whyte first published *The Social Life of Small Urban Spaces* in 1980; it was republished in 2001 by Project for Public Spaces, www.pps.org.

### CHAPTER 5: SHOP ON THE STREET

1. Downtown Denver Partnership, August 25, 2010. "16th Street Mall Urban Design Plan Public Meeting Presentation."

2. Interview with Cassie Milestone, Urban Planning Manager, Downtown Denver Partnership, February 2011.

3. Interview with John Desmond, Director, Downtown Denver Partnership, March 2015.

4. Gary Tung, "Mountain View, California: Fiat Res Publica," Places, Volume 5, Number 4. Permalink: http://escholarship.org/uc/item/8rp0k7b6.

5. Interview with Eric Anderson, City of Mountain View, February 2011.

6. Interviews with David Rasp, owner of Heroes Sports Bar and Grille, and Elizabeth Sanders, Downtown Mobile Alliance, February 2015.

7. Jason Bacaj, "Clocking in...with Jay Blaske, Food Truck Owner," Bozeman Daily Chronicle, June 25, 2013.

8. Interview with Jay Blaske, February 2014.

**CHAPTER 6: PLAY ON THE STREET**

1. J. P. Shonkoff, D. A. Phillips, eds. *From Neurons to Neighborhoods: The Science of Early Childhood Development* (Washington, D.C.: National Academy Press, 2000).

 Kenneth Ginsburg, M.D., M.S.Ed., "The Importance of Play in Promoting Healthy Child Development and Maintaining Strong Parent-Child Bonds," *Pediatrics, Journal of the American Academy of Pediatrics,* 119, 1 (January 1, 2007): 182–191. Accessed October 27, 2015, http://pediatrics.aappublications.org/content/119/1/182.full#sec-1.

 J. L. Frost, "Neuroscience, Play and Brain Development" (paper presented at IPA/USA Triennial National Conference; Longmont, CO, June 18–21, 1998). Accessed October 27, 2015, www.eric.ed.gov/ERICDocs/data/ericdocs2/content_storage_01/0000000b/80/11/56/d6.pdf.

 C. S. Tamis-LeMonda, J. D. Shannon, N. J. Cabrera, M.E. Lamb, "Fathers and mothers at play with their 2- and 3-year-olds: contributions to language and cognitive development," *Child Development* 75, 6 (2004): 1806–1820.

2. Susan Goltsman, Daniel Iacofano and Robin Moore, *Play For All* (Berkeley, CA: MIG Communications, 1992).

3. Michael Southworth and Eran Ben-Joseph, *Streets and the Shaping of Towns and Cities* (Washington, DC: Island Press, 2003).

 Joop H. Kraay, "Woonerfs and Other Experiments in The Netherlands," *Built Environment,* 12, 1/2 (1986): 20-29.

 Julian Baggini, "Playable Cities: The City That Plays Together, Stays Together," *The Guardian.* Accessed January 27, 2015, http://www.theguardian.com/cities/2014/sep/04/playable-cities-the-city-that-plays-together-stays-together.

4. Hettie Fox and Lyman Place, interview and site visit by Mukul Malhotra, New York, June 2014.

 David Gonzalez, "Play Street Becomes a Sanctuary," *New York Times,* July 31, 2009. Accessed January 27, 2015, http://www.nytimes.com/2009/08/02/nyregion/02ritual.html?pagewanted=1&ref=summerrituals.

 "Bronx Woman's Goal: Revive a Block," *New York Times,* July 24, 1988. Accessed January 27, 2015, http://www.nytimes.com/1988/07/24/nyregion/bronx-woman-s-goal-revive-a-block.html.

 "Your Friendly Neighborhood Power Brokers," *Transportation Alternatives,* (Spring 2011). Accessed January 27, 2015, http://www.transalt.org/newsroom/magazine/2011/Spring/1.

 Mike Lanza, "Investing in Kids' Play," *Playborhood* (June 30, 2010). Accessed January 27, 2015, http://playborhood.com/2010/06/investing_in_kids_play/ (Lanza 2014b).

Mike Lanza, "It Takes a Street to Raise Jacob," *Playborhood* (August 6, 2010). Accessed January 27, 2015, http://playborhood.com/2010/08/it_takes_a_street_to_raise_jacob/.

5. You can watch a video of the neighborhood at https://www.youtube.com/watch?v=WawJKtvVHKs. More information from the BBC News, accessed at http://news.bbc.co.uk/2/hi/uk_news/england/oxfordshire/8498171.stm.

6. More information at theurbanconga.com. The project was funded in part by KaBOOM!, a nonprofit that brings play to disadvantaged children; kaboom.org.

7. Silvia Pettem, "History of Pearl Street," *Downtown Boulder Inc.* (2014). Accessed January 27, 2015, http://www.boulderdowntown.com/visit/history-of-pearl-street.

8. Luke Jerram, *Urban Slide*. Accessed January 28, 2015, http://www.lukejerram.com/projects/urban_slide.

"Bristol giant water slide sees thrill-seekers soaked," *BBC News,* May 4, 2014. Accessed January 27, 2015, http://www.bbc.com/news/uk-england-bristol-27274501.

9. Luke Jerram, "Play Me, I'm Yours," *Street Pianos.* Accessed January 28, 2015, http://www.streetpianos.com.

10. Michael Levenson, "Rose Fitzgerald Kennedy Greenway Draws Increasing Crowds as It Becomes People's Park," *BostonGlobe.com*. Accessed October 22, 2014, https://www.bostonglobe.com/metro/2013/08/17/rose-fitzgerald-kennedy-greenway-draws-increasing-crowds-becomes-people-park/5gTs1YwnXy22ANvAeNrYrL/story.html.

"Greenway History," Rose Kennedy Greenway Conservancy. Accessed October 22, 2014, http://www.rosekennedygreenway.org/about-us/greenway-history/.

**CHAPTER 7: GROW ON THE STREET**

1. "The Western Diet Really IS a Killer: People Who Eat White Bread, Butter and Red Meat Are Most Likely to Die Young," *Mail Online*. Accessed October 24, 2014, http://www.dailymail.co.uk/health/article-2310053/The-Western-diet-really-IS-killer-People-eat-white-bread-butter-red-meat-likely-die-young.html.

2. "The History of Urban Agriculture Should Inspire Its Future," *Grist*. Accessed October 23, 2014, http://grist.org/article/food-the-history-of-urban-agriculture-should-inspire-its-future/.

3. Jillian Burt, "The Blade Runner Cookbook," *Huffington Post*. Accessed September 3, 2010, http://www.huffingtonpost.com/jillian-burt/the-blade-runner-cookbook_b_688695.html.

4. Dickson Despommier, "The Vertical Farm—Feeding the World in the 21st Century—with Dickson Despommier." Accessed October 27, 2014, http://www.verticalfarm.com/.

5. Robert Barrs, "Sustainable Urban Food Production in the City of Vancouver: An Analytical and Strategy

Framework for Planners and Decision-Makers." Accessed June 29, 2002, http://www.cityfarmer.org/barrsUAvanc.html.

**6.** Brad Lancaster, interview January 2015; visit www.desertharvesters.org for more information. The City of Tucson now requires new and reconstructed roads to be designed to harvest the first 1/2 inch of water; visit www.desertharvesters.org for more information.

**7.** Site visit conducted by Mukul Malhotra, July 2012.

**8.** Jeffrey Betcher, Quesada Gardens Initiative, site visit and interview, June 30, 2011.

**9.** Shelah Moody, "Jefferson Awards: Karl Paige and Annette Smith: Quesada Avenue Neighbors Transform a Dismal Median Strip into Bright Oasis," Accessed October 15, 2014, http://www.sfgate.com/bayarea/article/JEFFERSON-AWARDS-Karl-Paige-and-Annette-Smith-2539141.php.

**10.** Brigette Meinhold, "Pasona HQ is an Urban Farm That Grows Food for Its Employees in Tokyo." Accessed February 27, 2013, http://inhabitat.com/pasona-hq-is-an-urban-farm-that-grows-food-for-its-employees-in-tokyo/.

**11.** Kate Andrews, "Pasona Urban Farm by Kono Designs." Accessed March 25, 2015, http://www.dezeen.com/2013/09/12/pasona-urban-farm-by-kono-designs/.

**12.** Mark Francis, "Village Homes: A Case Study in Community Design," *Landscape Journal* 21:1-02 (2002): 23–41.

**13.** Thomas Lenz, "A Post-Occupancy Evaluation of Village Homes, Davis, California," unpublished Masters Thesis, Technical University of Munich (1990).

**14.** Eleanor Lewis, "The 21st Century Victory Garden," National Garden Bureau. Accessed March 26, 2015, http://ngb.org/todays_garden/index.cfm?TGID=15.

**15.** National Gardening Association, "The Impact of Home and Community Gardening in America." Accessed January 5, 2015, http://www.gardenresearch.com/files/2009-Impact-of-Gardening-in-America-White-Paper.pdf.

**CHAPTER 8: GENERATE ON THE STREET**

**1.** In a report by Daniel Hoornweg and Perinaz Bhada-Tata, "What a Waste: A Global Review of Solid Waste," produced by the World Bank as part of its Urban Development series, available at http://go.worldbank.org.

**2.** In Brazil recycling has been accepted as a legitimate profession, and workers don't need to supply things that informals may not have, like a street address, an identity card or a bank account. The City of Pune, India created micro collection and recycling zones for informal workers. The City provides health insurance, and the workers have formed a union, which designed a wet-dry source separation protocol. The system is based on a minimal form contract, and a standard for calculating service tariffs. Service fees are paid directly by the households to a service provider whom they know personally, and who has the right to value and sell both the dry recyclables and the organic waste. In Lima, Peru, the City provides uniforms, gloves, and transport equipment, and the informals have the right to the materials they pick up. They accept a sub-minimum wage from the City, and get to keep the proceeds of selling the materials—which also reduces the City's solid waste budget. And informal junk shops function as materials recovery facilities, buying and selling the recycled materials.

The study is in "The Economics of the Informal Sector in Solid Waste Management," by Ellen Gunsilius, Bharati Chaturvedi, Anne Scheinberg, with contributions from Adrian Coad, Sofia Garcia Cortes, published in 2011 by CWG (Collaborative Working Group on Solid Waste Management in Low- and Middle-income Countries), GIZ - Deutsche Gesellschaft für Internationale Zusammenarbeit (GIZ) GmbH, www.cwgnet.net.

3. More information at pollinatorpathway.com.

4. You can find native plants by area at plants.usda. gov and at wildflower.org. The University of Bristol is conducting an in-depth study of urban pollinators; more information at Bristol.ac.uk/biology/research/ ecological/community/pollinators.

5. More information available at solaroad.nl/en.

6. The City of Chicago has developed Sustainable Urban Infrastructure Guidelines, available at cityofchicago. org/cdot, then search for the guide. More information about the Pilsen Sustainable Street at ward25.com/ sustainable-streetscapes-green-alleys.

7. The City provides guidelines, stormwater manuals, case studies, videos and more information at portlandoregon.gov/bes/44407.

8. Online interview with Ivy Dunlap, Stormwater System Division, City of Portland, December 2015.

9. More information about at DOLL and its other initiatives at lightinglab.dk/UK. One of the technologies being tested is Tvilight, developed in the Netherlands. It includes sophisticated sensors that can be attached to new or existing lights and that can dynamically provide on-demand lighting for the different speeds of cars, pedestrians and bicyclists. Emergency vehicles can turn lights red to alert people before they hear a siren.

10. More information available at habitatsteppingstones. org.au.

11. More information at noordforce.com.

12. More information at Ooms.nl.

13. More information and a diagram is in the September 2015 issue of Asia Research News and in Asian

Scientist, November 2015, asianscientist.com/2015/11/ tech/street-lamp-targets-dengue-fever. Or contact the developer directly: Dr. Chong Wen Tong, Department of Mechanical Engineering, University of Malaysia, 50603 Kuala Lumpur, Malaysia, chong_wentong@ um.edu.my.

**14.** More information about the Olive Center and olives in general at olivecenter.ucdavis.edu.

**15.** The bridge has been standing for almost 10 years; more information at http://viterbi.usc.edu/news/news/2007/ astani-department-engineer.htm.

**Streets Reconsidered** | Inclusive Design for the Public Realm

reStreets.org
MIGcom.com
800-790-8444